Shadow
OF THE KNIGHT

Shadow
OF THE KNIGHT

FOLLOWING IN THE FOOTSTEPS OF SIR ALEX FERGUSON

PAUL SMITH

DEDICATION

To Coral, Finlay, Mia and Zara

First published by Pitch Publishing 2012

Pitch Publishing
A2 Yeoman Gate
Yeoman Way
Durrington
BN13 3QZ
www.pitchpublishing.co.uk

ISBN 978-1-90805-181-3

Typesetting and origination by Pitch Publishing.

Printed in Great Britain by TJ International.

Contents

Acknowledgements

S O MANY stories to tell, so many people to thank. A number of people lent their time and expertise to help me along the way as I negotiated my path through *Shadow of the Knight*, from lending advice to adding their anecdotes about life alongside Sir Alex Ferguson. Former players including Willie Garner, Neale Cooper, Charlie Nicholas and Neil Cooper were good enough to recall their experiences while one of his Pittodrie successors, Alex Smith, did likewise to paint a picture of the challenges facing all who have followed in Ferguson's footsteps. Duncan Shearer, a one-time Ferguson trialist and later a Pittodrie goalscoring legend, also provided his unique insight.

From Alex Donohue and Mark Young, two men of the turf, to journalist colleagues Jim Dolan, Phil Rostron and Arthur McTague, I was fortunate to have many friends to call upon. Paul and Jane Camillin at Pitch Publishing had the faith in the concept initially and the drive to follow it through to fruition, while closer to home the love and support of Team Smith – Coral, Finlay, Mia and baby Zara – never ceases to amaze and delight.

My heartfelt thanks go to all those mentioned above and the many others behind the scenes who helped along the way.

Introduction

THERE ARE very few individuals in football who could be classed as irreplaceable. Players come and players go, even those who displayed unabashed genius at their peak have a shelf life. George Best and Bobby Charlton at Manchester United, or more recently Roy Keane and David Beckham, all at one stage or other gave the impression the world would stop turning if they were not in a red shirt. They moved on, life moved on and the world kept turning. Memories will never be erased, but there will always be a new generation ready to make their mark and ease the pain of separation.

But what about the manager? Sir Alex Ferguson has been Manchester United for more than 25 years, the beating heart of one of the greatest clubs on the planet. From the smallest detail to the biggest signings, the influence of the man at the top spreads from the very top to the very bottom at Old Trafford and the training centre at Carrington.

It will be impossible to replace that, in a way that the club has never encountered before and never will again. No matter who walks through the front door to pick up the baton when Ferguson eventually calls time on his life and times at United, they will simply not be able to exert the same authority. The reason, quite simply, is time.

Over more than quarter of a century the football club has been moulded around Ferguson. It is his vision and his determination that has seen it become a giant both on and off the park. The next incumbent will be able to build a team, but the hard work in building the club to its position as a global brand has already been done.

But the manager will have to be replaced and his team and his club will have to move on. Managing that transition will be the toughest process anyone at Manchester United has gone through in modern times, certainly since the last new boss arrived in 1986 to embark upon his adventure in English football.

Then, the only way was up for a major team in need of major success to match its status. Today, the opposite is true – exceeding the standards and success of the incumbent regime will be a tall order.

There will be no shortage of volunteers though, enticed by the prospect of working with the ingredients so painstakingly gathered by Ferguson. He will, eventually, leave behind a squad with the exuberance of youth and the enormous benefit of experience in almost equal measure. It is a recipe he has proved so adept at creating throughout his managerial career.

When the dust settles on an incredible career at the top level, the legacy will stretch far beyond the confines of Old Trafford. The reach of Sir Alex is long, with his influence evident in all corners of Britain and on foreign shores through his work with so many people in every sphere. From the man back in Aberdeen who pioneered video analysis, to the high-profile coaches who have leapt from United to the international scene, the net can be spread wide.

Shadow of the Knight examines the task facing those at Old Trafford as they consider the next step. Appointing his successor would be akin to negotiating a minefield for the Old Trafford board while for the chosen man it represents an incredible challenge. The bookmakers already have an idea of which direction the power brokers will turn, while Sir Alex himself has made his views known about the type of character required.

The Damned United famously played out the perils of following in the footsteps of a powerful and successful manager steeped in the heritage of a club. Who will be the Brian Clough to Old Trafford's equivalent of Don Revie? Opinions vary, but familiar names are often repeated.

Perhaps they will surprise us by looking closer to home. There are candidates at Old Trafford and recently departed who would offer continuity, but it would represent a risk.

After all, not all of Ferguson's proteges have gone on to replicate his success despite tutelage by the master.

Whoever is chosen, they will have to live with the presence of a legend. Ferguson can be seen as stubborn – but equally as a genius. He will cast a shadow over United long after he has retired, the trick will be in ensuring the influence is used positively.

That is something Aberdeen have struggled to do in the decades since their most famous boss moved south. By looking at the experiences at Pittodrie, on and off the park, since 1986 it is possible to draw parallels between then and now in the context of the bitter experiences of the past quarter of a century and the way in which a succession of highly qualified men have struggled to break free from the comparisons with the Fergie years.

Incredibly it is almost 20 years since the Dons last won a trophy of any description. That coincides with Ferguson's absence, save for a handful of sporadic triumphs in the years after his departure.

The big question in the north-east of Scotland, an area he inspired with years of football success never seen before or since, is whether his legacy at Pittodrie was one of unrealistic expectation or a determination to strive for high standards.

Finding the players and manager capable of coping with that unique set of circumstances is something the Dons have struggled to do – presumably Manchester United, with the financial clout of a mega-club, will have less of an issue.

Trying to find someone with the same breadth of man-management skills will be the biggest challenge, to take charge of a dressing room full of strong characters.

Ferguson has thrived on getting the best out of some of the most complex individuals in football, never shirking a challenge.

Whether trying to shield David Beckham from the spotlight of superstardom or dealing with the Ryan Giggs meltdown, Ferguson learnt that aspect of his trade during his time at Pittodrie when he handled some equally controversial characters in less high profile surroundings.

From his fall-outs with Dons hero Joe Harper to run-ins with star man Steve Archibald, the lessons have been varied. That isn't to say he has passed the test every time, whether in man-management or in the transfer market.

There have been slips along the way, worth highlighting and recounting in any account of an incredible career.

That career began in very different times to those we live in now and it has taken in too many individuals to mention. However, it is worth considering some of those who were left behind – either by choice or as a result of Ferguson's ruthless pursuit of perfection. By tracking down some of those who fell by the wayside, I got a unique insight into the workings of the manager's mind and the regrets some of those who encountered him have.

His former Aberdeen assistant manager Willie Garner now works in financial services, and another former Pittodrie right-hand man, Pat Stanton, retired soon after parting company in amicable fashion.

With that in mind, what does the future hold for the close allies at Old Trafford who will be cut free from the security of their revered former boss? Time will tell.

Similarly, by talking to those who played alongside him in his younger days, and those who played under him in his time as a rookie coach, it is easy to get a sense of the traits which have helped him along the way.

My own father played alongside Ferguson at Rangers and was encouraged by his friend to enter management. Both had success to different degrees, but one lasted the distance and went right the way to the top. The reasons for that are explored in the pages that follow. Ferguson was an ordinary man with a dream – the difference is he went out and lived it.

From the grittiest beginnings at humble East Stirling, he worked tirelessly to ensure he would one day enjoy the fruits of his labour on the muddy training fields of the lower leagues.

He has, however, never forgotten those he encountered on his climb through the ranks.

As many members of the old boys network were quick to tell me, his friendship lasts a lifetime and can come to the rescue at the most vital of times.

That ranges from impromptu coaching stints for former Dons players down on their luck to loan deals to farm players out to his old club or former colleagues and the decision to send teams across the country to play in testimonials in honour of close allies and, most recently, his son during his start in life as a manager in his own right.

Darren Ferguson will continue the family's work on the front line of football for years to come.

That is, of course, assuming that Sir Alex does eventually retire – and, if he does, is not tempted back in by the back door. Would the call of his country bring him back to the international scene he left behind in 1986, when he led Scotland in the World Cup finals in Mexico? When eventually free of club commitments, he is sure to be linked.

But then he already has his hands full with life as a racehorse owner, charity supporter, family man and a global sporting superstar.

Having spoken to so many people who have had their lives touched by football's own knight of the realm, it is difficult to imagine there will not be many more captivating chapters to be written.

Chapter 1

LET'S START with a confession. I'm not a betting man, never have been, never will be. But who better to turn to for an answer to one of life's imponderables than a bookmaker? After all, the bookie is never wrong. In any case, given his love of the racing game then surely Sir Alex himself would approve of the less than scientific approach to answering the big question: who is going to be the next manager of Manchester United?

Ask the question and the general response is furrowed brows all around. In fact, the suggestion that Manchester United will in fact have another manager, one day, is met with incredulity in certain quarters. I set the teaser as the dust settled on the incredible 2011/12 season, days after Sir Alex's troops had been pipped at the post by Manchester City in the most dramatic of circumstances. Yet still the response was the same – the next manager at Old Trafford was not imminent. There was life in the old dog yet.

But, ever dependable, the bookies have still got it covered. Just in case. Buried deep in a pile of carefully compiled odds on things that may never happen, just beneath the first man to walk on Mars and on top of the first Liberal Democrat prime minister is a dusty list of potential replacements for the undisputed godfather of football management.

Top of the list, across the board, was a certain Jose Mourinho. The self-titled Special One even had the endorsement of Sir Alex as a potential heir to the throne, in a roundabout way, but then he went and ruined it all by signing a new four-year contract with Real Madrid in May 2012. All bets were off, quite literally, as bookmakers hastily shut down the section of their websites dedicated to the Manchester United succession plan for a hasty rethink on the runners and riders.

Pep Guardiola, clear of his Barcelona commitments, was another of the favoured candidates while Red Devils hero Ole Gunnar Solskjaer was another high on the odds list after an impressive start to managerial life with Molde in Norway. Martin O'Neill, the saviour of Sunderland, was also mentioned in dispatches alongside a succession with Old Trafford links: Laurent Blanc, Steve Bruce, Mark Hughes were all there in the top ten with the wily Scot of Goodison, David Moyes, also included. Then there was Ryan Giggs, the man who had sparked a run of betting early in 2012 when he was tipped as a future manager by both Ferguson and team-mate Paul Scholes.

The scattergun approach from those who make their living from second-guessing the big events in the world of sport demonstrated one thing – knowing which way Manchester United will look for their next boss is almost impossible to predict. There's even a good-going business in taking bets on when the most momentous retirement in football will take place, with wagers being taken that Ferguson's career with Manchester United would stretch past his 75th birthday in 2016. Only time will tell whether that is a punt that pays out.

Going into the 2012/13 season, Mourinho remained top of the pile according to the experts at Ladbrokes. The man from Portugal was rated 5/2 for the Old Trafford job, followed closely by the unemployed Guardiola at 9/2. Then came the less exotic but nonetheless plausible contenders, with Moyes at 6/1 as the bookies clearly considered the possibility of a man cut from similar cloth as Sir Alex being appointed his successor. Like Ferguson, Moyes had not had a world-beating playing career but, like Ferguson, he had worked his socks off to make a go of his opportunities in management. Like Ferguson his blood runs tartan.

Next on the table of likely lads was Gary Neville, rated 10/1 alongside Martin O'Neill and Ole Gunnar Solskjaer. Neville, part of Roy Hodgson's England set-up by then, would be a logical but incredibly risky appointment, given his lack of front line experience. Clearly he would have the respect of those he had served alongside in the trenches, but from a hard-headed business point of view he would struggle to match the more established contenders.

According to the men of the turf, England's performance in Euro 2012 was a key factor in determining the likelihood of Neville earning a fast-track to Old Trafford's seat of power. Had Neville and company gone on to win in Poland and Ukraine, then their erstwhile young coach would have been a hero. As it happened, the curse of penalties struck and the more modest quarter-final exit at the hands of Italy diluted the case. It was a respectable performance, but not one to capture the imagination.

Ryan Giggs, at 14/1 on the same list, would fall into the same category as his former team-mate – but was still rated ahead of the big hitters on the 20/1 mark. Fabio Capello and Guus Hiddink were joined by Old Trafford legend Mark Hughes at that price. Hughes may have been higher had it not been for a shaky start to life with QPR and the blot on his copybook from his defection to the blue half of Manchester for his brief flirtation with City.

The old boys network features highly in the bookies' list of contenders, perhaps suggesting they feel Sir Alex himself may have an influence on the succession plan. Assistant manager Mike Phelan sits at 25/1 while former skipper Roy Keane, no friend of Ferguson in recent years, joins his former midfield partner Paul Scholes at 33/1.

How about the outside shot of Eric Cantona, listed at 40/1? Perhaps not a sound investment for your hard-earned pennies – there are safer names to plump for, according to the experts.

Alex Donohue, of Ladbrokes, is sure Mourinho will be the man when the time eventually comes. He said: "We've always held the Special One up as the man to eventually take over from Sir Alex Ferguson when he decides to retire.

"Along with Guardiola they seem to be head and shoulders above the field in terms of calibre and it's simply a case of them being in the right place when the vacancy arises."

With Guardiola stepping away from Barcelona, he thrust himself on to the market – albeit with his protestations that he was content to sit back and wait for the right opportunity to crop up. Tantalisingly, the man who created a football team that mirrored a work of art at the Nou Camp has hinted that a club of United's stature could tempt him back from his self-imposed football exile.

Speaking of the clubs expected to court him in the months ahead, the Spaniard said in the summer of 2012: "I will be pleased to receive their calls, but for the next months I have to charge my batteries and charge my mind.

"I will wait. I am going to rest and I will wait. I will be ready once a club want me. If they seduce me I will train again."

Roma tried to seduce him, but failed. Could Manchester United succeed where the Italians had failed? There was every chance, since Guardiola himself had suggested England would be his next destination.

He would be a high profile export, but the smattering of coaches located closer to home would have something to say about the need for the Old Trafford chiefs to cast their net quite so wide. Of the home-grown options, two men stand out from the crowd as far as the Ladbrokes expert is concerned. Donohue added: "David Moyes has been touted for quite some time and has been an ever-present in our odds list, however, the big market mover in recent times is Gary Neville, who saw his odds slashed from 66/1 to 10/1 on the back of his England appointment. It's a clear sign of his maturity and intent."

Two notable old boys missing from the most recent odds list are one-time assistants Steve McClaren and Carlos Queiroz. The latter, in particular, was a hot tip for the top job – touted by none other than Ferguson himself.

Speaking during a question and answer session at the Citizens Theatre in Glasgow in 2007, while the Portuguese coach was still by his side, Ferguson said: "Thankfully, I don't have to make the decision. I have a great assistant in Carlos Queiroz, I think he will be a strong candidate. We have new owners now and I don't know how they look at the situation over in America. They have been great supporters of everything we have done but they may have their own ideas."

The timing of the departure is likely to be led by the man himself. He will know when it is time to go, surely unthinkable that anyone else would make the decision.

Speaking on the subject of retirement, Ferguson said: "The thing is I have not made my mind up when I'm retiring. It's a difficult one. It's not going to be an easy decision. The important thing is to leave a good team."

He has been over the course before, coming to the decision to retire before performing a u-turn. In the same theatre talk-in, he added: "I had won the European Cup, I wanted to leave a good team. But it's difficult when you get to that stage and you have been there that long, when you choose the moment to retire. One New Year's Day with the family we all went for lunch and I was dozing on the couch when the boss came in and kicked my feet and said 'you're not retiring'. The three sons were sitting behind her and what could I do?"

So he continued, soldiering on with a job to do and no sign of letting up. But success, or a lack of it, could have a huge part to play in when the inevitable departure occurs.

William Hill offered a price of 4/7 on Manchester United to finish the 2012/13 season without a trophy – and a huge 300/1 for Ferguson's men to win the clean sweep domestically and in Europe. More realistically, it seemed, was the prospect of something in between. Reigning champions Manchester City were favourites for the Premiership prize, with United at 5/2 and expected to be breathing down their neck.

Mark Young, of William Hill, told me: "Manchester United were viewed as having a great chance going into the new season, considering it was only goal difference that cost them in 2011/12 – but City were always expected to spend and improve an already talented squad."

Manchester United's spending was, at one time, huge. Rio Ferdinand, Jaap Stam, Ruud van Nistelrooy...the list goes on. In recent years that time of grandstanding has been pulled right in, with Ferguson having to box clever and make every signing count.

According to Young, there's no sign of the ability to unearth gems fading with age. He added: "The signing of Shinji Kagawa was exciting at Old Trafford and another example of Fergie getting his man. More improvement is needed but United will always be there or there about, fighting City and probably Chelsea."

So there we have it, the experts have spoken. We don't know when it will happen, or quite how, but one day soon Manchester United will have to face up to life after Sir Alex Ferguson.

Who steps into the void is a mystery, but the odds stack up to suggest that it will take a powerful character to emerge from the shadow of the knight. As the man himself once said: "I hope and expect they will be a formidable persona, because this job, believe me, is not easy."

None comes more formidable than Mourinho – and the fact he himself has done nothing to extinguish the flickering embers of speculation. Speaking to BBC Radio Four's *Today* programme in 2011, Mourinho admitted: "I am very, very happy to be in Real Madrid. It is a great experience for me. I believe it is probably the biggest club in the history of football, I didn't want to miss the chance to work here, but my passion is England and my next step will be to go back, if possible go and stay for a long time. Get me a club in a couple of years, get me a good club."

A good club? A Chelsea return perhaps. Or maybe a cross-city switch to Arsenal. Or the lure of an open chequebook at Manchester City. But more likely than any of those is a call to arms from Old Trafford, and the Special One is ready for that call.

Speaking in 2009, while serving Inter Milan, he said: "I would consider going to Manchester United but United have to consider if they want me to succeed Sir Alex Ferguson. If they do, then of course."

Mourinho may have been brought up a world away, or at least, the bulk of a continent away, from Sir Alex's roots in Govan but they do share a common bond of a football education in the Scottish west coast town of Largs.

Ferguson went through his coaching badges under the auspices of the Scottish Football Association and so too did Mourinho, who made the unusual decision to leave his home country behind in favour of being put through his paces at the SFA classes.

In many ways their football philosophy is similar, with the younger of the two understanding the elder statesman's staying power.

Mourinho said: "This is an amazing experience – many of us don't want to quit, ever. We want to go to the last day we can because this leadership becomes part of our life."

And what has become part of Mourinho's life, as it has for Sir Alex, is working with some of the most naturally gifted men the world of football has ever seen.

CHAPTER 1

The man from Portugal said: "I think the genius will make always the difference. And the genius in my sport is about some unbelievable players that can break every organisation and every work you can do. Genius in managing also exists. For me, the most important thing is man-management. Football for me is a human science, it is about man.

"Emotional intelligence is crucial at this level in every sport. It is one thing to take a penalty winning 5-0 in a friendly, another thing is to take a penalty kick in the last minute of the Champions League or World Cup final. I try to prepare my players the best I can but at the end of the day they are the guys that decide everything in the right moment. They make the difference. I analyse them in a group context always but I know they are all unique."

Mourinho's strong character, supreme self-confidence and forthright opinions provide a shield against the criticism that invariably accompanies top level appointments. The perfect set of armoury for a job at a club on Manchester United's level and for replacing a man of Sir Alex Ferguson's stature.

There are echoes of history repeating itself. Remember *The Damned United*? It was Leeds back then, but could quite easily be Manchester in the modern game. Don Revie was a managerial behemoth who had to be replaced by a big character and Brian Clough was that man. The solution to the problem did, quite famously, end in failure. Whether the same thing would happen at Old Trafford if Mourinho were to take the helm is something author and journalist Phil Rostron has given some thought.

Rostron, who penned the book *We Are The Damned United*, charting the facts of life at Leeds United under Brian Clough as an antidote to the fiction hit *The Damned United*, said: "I can see a link between the two situations. Leeds were faced with replacing a very powerful manager, just as Manchester United will be when Alex Ferguson eventually retires. Leeds had some very influential players who had their own ideas about the direction the club should take, just as Manchester United do today. Supporters of the club have to hope that when it does happen, the transition goes far more smoothly than it did at Elland road.

"The players nurtured within Revie's caring and disciplined environment, those who made up the team and whose names tripped off the tongue of even the most befuddled drunk in Whitelocks, the city of Leeds' favourite alehouse – Sprake, Reaney, Cooper, Bremner, Charlton, Hunter, Lorimer, Clarke, Jones, Giles, Gray – loved Revie to a man. He drove them mad sometimes with his idiosyncratic behaviour – the superstitions, the fussy attention to detail, his daft bonding games such as carpet bowls – but they adored his father-figure persona and the family atmosphere created by the boss and his wife Elsie.

"So who would replace him? Was it possible to replace him? Certainly, not least in the minds of the squad he left behind, it needed to be someone of great stature. Johnny Giles, United's midfield brainbox, was overwhelmingly the dressing-room vote. Surely, though, any manager worth his salt would climb over dead bodies to take over England's reigning champions. Billy Bremner, the heart of Revie's squad, threw his hat into the ring. The guessing game went on into the early hours in many a household. One name was unconsidered: Brian Clough. He despised Leeds. Didn't like their departing manager. Had publicly called them cheats. No way."

But as we all know, that's exactly the direction the Leeds board took at that juncture. And we all also know the unhappy outcome for all concerned.

Rostron added: "Where Revie had gone to great lengths to explain what he required of his players, a rather more succinct overview of Clough's management mantra can be found in the manager's player rule-book in place during Clough and Taylor's time at Derby. On the one hand, a caring, arm-round approach; on the other a hard-hitting list of don't-dos. Come what may, there was going to be a stark change in the atmosphere at Elland Road. The appointment promised to be interesting."

Rostron's book looks at the Clough appointment through the eyes of the Leeds United players, rather than those of the manager himself. What shines through in the observations is the sense of loss those players felt, to a man, when Revie departed. A huge hole was ripped out of the heart of the club that day and filling that void would have been impossible – just as replacing Alex Ferguson would be at Old Trafford.

What the Leeds board had to try and do was come up with the next best solution – and, according to the players, the solution should have been closer to home than the board appeared prepared to look.

Eddie Gray told Rostron: "The general belief in the camp was that the job at Leeds would go to Johnny Giles. Indeed, he had been told he had got it. We were out on Fullerton Park kicking a ball about one afternoon and Johnny came up to Peter Lorimer and I and said: 'I'm the new manager.' Then it was discovered that somebody else in the camp had put in an application. That someone else was Billy Bremner. Billy, of course, was a big character at the club and quite within his rights to apply for the job, but here, now, was a dilemma for the board. I think the chairman, Manny Cussins, and his board were wary about running the risk of having a split camp."

That threat of a split applies to any club where an internal appointment is considered, something that directors have to take into account. External candidates offer a clean break, a politically neutral option and one that is understandably attractive.

The internal politics are something that come to the fore with every managerial change and, taking lessons from the past, the Manchester United hierarchy would be advised to ensure they treat their departing man with the respect he deserves.

Peter Hampton, a squad man at Leeds at the time of Revie's departure, told Rostron: "I was only on the fringe of things and, where one or two people were probably initially in the know, I had got no inkling. All of a sudden, he's gone and got the England job. If the chance to manage your country is offered, then you're going to take it, aren't you? But I've gone through life believing that the directors of Leeds United never gave Don the credit for what he did and what he achieved, and that may have played a part in his decision-making process. They always thought, I feel, that it was down to them, and not Revie, that Leeds had done so well.

"Directors are like that, though, aren't they? Always have been. It's that blazer mentality. It was without a shadow of a doubt Don Revie who built, engineered and crafted the great Leeds of the 1960s and 1970s. His choice and treatment of his staff, his empathy with his players and his acquisitions were spot-on. He was truly one of the greats. Yet in modern-day pontifications and summaries about the giants of our game, he is never mentioned, and that, to me, is both surprising and shocking.

"The obvious thing for the directors to have done when Revie left was to appoint John Giles as his successor. That is what I would have done and it was what many of the players wanted."

The players didn't get what they wanted though, they got the complete opposite. The result was disastrous. Maybe, just maybe, those with the biggest decision in the history of Manchester United should be looking within to find the answer to the momentous question: who is man enough to step out of the shadow of the knight?

Chapter 2

The last time Sir Alex Ferguson left a club, he was offered the keys to the door as an incentive to change his mind. Nobody will ever know if the Aberdeen FC chairman of the time, the late Dick Donald, was serious with his offer to gift his talismanic manager the Dons – what is certain is that he had done enough in his eight years at Pittodrie to merit weighty encouragement to reverse his decision to depart for Manchester United.

Comparisons between Aberdeen and Manchester United are difficult to make. They are two very different beasts. The Dons were, during the Ferguson-inspired glory days, a provincial club punching well above its weight. Today it remains a provincial club, but one that stands accused of underperforming.

Manchester United were, before the Ferguson-inspired revival, a sleeping giant that had failed to match its potential. After benefiting from his Midas touch, the club has been transformed into a global institution, steeped in success at home and abroad and supporting a business machine that puts the Red Devils in a league of their own.

There are, however, parallels to be drawn. Both play in red, both have been spurred on by a certain man from Govan – and both have had to face up to the idea of somehow replacing that great figurehead. United have been able to put that conundrum on the back burner for longer than Aberdeen were able to, only pausing from time to time when it looked as though the Red Devils boss was ready to ride off into the sunset, but it would be naive to think the US owners have not thought long and hard about the succession plan. With the huge financial weight of the Manchester United machine behind them, nobody is off limits for the power brokers. The world is indeed their oyster.

Aberdeen, on the other hand, had to be slightly more pragmatic in their approach, without the back-up of a turnover running into hundreds of millions of pounds. They were, thanks to the trophy-laden years under Ferguson's guidance, well enough heeled and in a position to pay well for players and managers but, under the canny stewardship of Donald and his vice-chairman Chris Anderson, there was never the prospect of reckless spending in a bid to offset the loss of the man who had done more than any other individual to put Aberdeen on football's map.

Regardless of finance, they faced the same considerations as Manchester United: how to solve a problem like Fergie? Do you attempt to replace like with like? Finding a domineering and all-seeing manager in the Ferguson mould is difficult, but not impossible. Or do you take the approach that a change is as good as a rest – look for a softer option? Or do you look internally for a populist choice, promote from within in a bid to win fans' favour and earn vital breathing space? Aberdeen, in the end, drove a line somewhere down the middle of those three.

Every man and his dog appeared to have been linked with the Pittodrie post, with interest stoked by the potential to work with the star-studded cast left behind by Ferguson.

Archie Knox had turned down the chance to stay on as manager in his own right, choosing to follow his friend to England and continue in his role as assistant manager, and two names dominated the headlines as the hunt for Ferguson's successor began: Sandy Jardine and Willie Miller.

Miller, Aberdeen's legendary captain, was an obvious candidate, even though he still had several seasons as a player in front of him, while Jardine, assistant to Alex McDonald at Hearts, was the departing manager's own recommendation to the Aberdeen board. Jardine had been a team-mate of Ferguson's during his Rangers days, a cultured player who had been earning a reputation as an emerging coach at Tynecastle. It was an interesting tip from the departing manager, one worthy of consideration.

When Ian Porterfield was revealed as the choice it came as a bolt from the blue, it was an appointment nobody had predicted. He had emerged from the blind-side as the board's first choice to take over and he was appointed swiftly after his first meeting with directors.

Although a Scot by birth, having launched his playing career with Raith Rovers, he had spent the bulk of his professional life in England after moving to Sunderland in 1967. He was the goalscoring hero as the Black Cats triumphed in the 1973 FA Cup Final against the mighty Leeds United, but within 18 months had his sporting life put in perspective when a car accident left him fighting for survival and battling to recover from a fractured skull. He did that, showing incredible grit and determination, and continued to play an important part for Sunderland before shifting to Sheffield Wednesday, serving as captain and player-coach under Jack Charlton. Porterfield was a promotion-winning manager with both Rotherham United and Sheffield United – where his efforts were rewarded with a ten-year contract. Despite that lengthy deal, he was dismissed by the Blades but bounced back in incredible style with the appointment at Aberdeen.

The Dons directors had clearly decided that replacing Ferguson was an impossibility. Rather than going for an identikit successor, they had gone for a man who arrived with no baggage and no weight of expectation. He had a blank canvas to work from, with no preconceived ideas about either the squad he had at his disposal or about Scottish football as a whole. Similar, on a far smaller scale, to the Chelsea experiment with Andre Villas-Boas.

Just as Roman Abramovich found to his huge cost, experiments come with no guarantees of success. The financial consequences may have been miniscule in comparison, but Aberdeen's directors had their fingers burnt with the Porterfield episode. He lasted just a season and a half in the hot-seat, still warm from the presence of the fiery Ferguson. He was a determined character, of that there could be no doubt, but Porterfield struggled to impose himself on a club and a city still heavily under the influence of his predecessor.

He quit the post on 16th May 1988 – five years, give or take a few days, from Ferguson's sensational triumph over Real Madrid with his plucky Dons side. Personal reasons were cited for Porterfield's departure, with the coach keen to take his children back to familiar territory in England, but disappointing results were undoubtedly a huge part of the problem. He had simply failed to emerge from Ferguson's shadow. That is not a slight on the individual, since any manager would have found it impossible to emulate Ferguson.

He had been joined at Aberdeen by assistant Jimmy Mullen, with the duo subsequently helped by the appointment of experienced campaigner Alex Smith as co-assistant manager to lend his valuable knowledge of the Scottish game. When it came to looking for a replacement for Porterfield, it was Smith the board turned to. He had seen at first hand the difficulties any Aberdeen manager would have in living with the expectations that had been hyped up by Ferguson's achievements. He accepted the challenge, but would find in later years that the expectations were not diluted with time.

Smith had already turned down the substantial lure of a coaching role at Rangers to commit to Aberdeen, recruited to assist Porterfield in an attempt to bridge the gap between club football north and south of the border. Little did he realise that within days of his appointment to the Pittodrie backroom team he would be handed one of the biggest club jobs in Scotland at that time.

Smith told me: "Initially I moved to Pittodrie to assist Ian along with Jimmy Mullen but within a week Ian had resigned. I had spent the week helping push Jim Leighton's transfer to Manchester United through, Ian didn't speak to Alex so I was involved in most of the talks. Then Ian left.

"I had been detailed to take the youth team to play in Switzerland and was taking them for my first training session on the university fields in Aberdeen. That team had the likes of Eoin Jess, David Robertson, Scott Booth and Stevie Gray – all great young players. During that session Jimmy came across and told me I had to report to the ground, the chairman wanted to speak to me. When I went back to Pittodrie, Mr Donald offered me the manager's job and told me to put together a management team.

"I asked Jocky Scott and Drew Jarvie to join me. Drew had been assistant to Jocky, who was manager at Dundee at the time. To tempt Jocky to come we decided to make it a co-managers' appointment because he was in charge in his own right at Dens. It allowed him to play an important role with the club and gave him a better platform for the future. I had to compromise a little bit with that but I knew Jocky was very good, as I knew with Drew. The three of us together made a very strong team."

Although benefiting from Porterfield's swift demise, Smith still has sympathy with the situation his predecessor found himself in when he arrived in the north-east. In fact, Smith had been one of the names on the speculative list of possible contenders prior to Porterfield's appointment. He has every right to be thankful his turn came later.

"There was a fair bit of pressure on Ian after coming in to replace Alex Ferguson. Although Alex's reign was starting to slip a bit by the time he left Aberdeen, he had started to do the Scotland job on a part-time basis and Manchester United had been looming for him, it was still an awful big act to follow.

"Certainly being the second manager after Alex was better than going in immediately because there was still a shadow when Ian arrived, although I suppose there will always be that shadow. Ian's team had a reasonably good record of consistency, they didn't score many goals but equally didn't concede many. They made two cup finals but lost both of them and that wasn't enough to match what had gone before."

The daunting task did not deter Smith from accepting the challenge presented to him, the biggest managerial break of his career. It was a realisation of the dream harboured since he started out on the first rung of the coaching ladder in 1968.

Smith admits: "There was no doubt it was a massive club, a European club with a dressing room full of international players, and a big job. Only a couple of years before they had won in Europe and even after that won a lot of domestic trophies. At the same time it was still very much a pro-family club. The directors, players, management, staff and fans were all part of one big family and that made it a good place to work."

Unlike Porterfield, and Ferguson before him, Smith had not played at the top level. His playing career took in the more humble surroundings of Stirling Albion, East Stirling, Albion Rovers and Stenhousemuir. He demonstrated a burning desire in management when he took charge of his first team at the age of 28 in 1968 with Stenhousemuir and never looked back.

Smith has often heralded the managerial apprenticeship he served at Stenny and then Stirling Albion, lamenting the speed with which players are being thrust into the pressure-cooker environment of top flight management in the modern game. Ultimately that trend cost him his Aberdeen job when Willie Miller was propelled into the manager's office after a short spell as a coach.

He shot to prominence as a manager with St Mirren when the Paisley side enjoyed its finest hour with victory over Dundee United in the Scottish Cup Final of 1987. Thanks to that momentous win, when it was time to part company with the Buddies there were no shortage of takers. It was Aberdeen who won his services.

Smith explained: "I had done a good job at St Mirren, both with the team and financially for the club. My departure was really political rather than anything else. We had won the Scottish Cup and Ian Ferguson was sold to Rangers for more than £1m. At the start of the cup run Steve Clarke had been sold for £450,000 to Chelsea.

"A new chairman came in and there were changes at board level. The harmony you need between manager and chairman wasn't there and it became clear it was time to move on. I found myself in the strange situation of having the Scottish Cup on the sideboard and near enough £1.6m in the club's bank account but looking for a new job.

"There were three offers at that stage. One was from the SFA and another from Rangers to head up their youth development programme, from the very youngest player right up to the edge of the first team. The third was from Aberdeen to go up and work with Ian Porterfield. The club thought because he had been working in England it would benefit him to work with someone who knew the Scottish game.

"Initially when I moved north to link up with Ian, I was encouraged by Willie Miller and Alex McLeish to take the job – they knew about the alternative offers I had and that I had the chance to go to Rangers but felt Aberdeen at that time needed a similar type as Alex Ferguson and Archie Knox on board. Myself, Alex and Archie, along with other Scottish coaches, work in similar patterns even though by nature we are all very different people. I think Willie and Alex, obviously the two most senior players at that time, wanted to keep the Scottish way of doing things because Ian was very Anglified in the way he ran the club."

With the support of the Dons heavyweights, the transition from coach to manager was made painless for Smith as he set about building on the foundations he found at Pittodrie. What he inherited was a mix of Ferguson's fragmenting Gothenburg team, those he had signed since that European triumph and the fresh blood added since Porterfield's arrival.

The rock-solid defensive partnership of Miller and McLeish remained intact, Neil Simpson was still patrolling the midfield and John Hewitt was still on hand when Smith took the reins. Ferguson's more recent acquisitions, the likes of Jim Bett and Stewart McKimmie, were to be key men in the new regime but Porterfield's recruits had a shorter stay.

Only the mercurial talents of Charlie Nicholas were to prove of real worth to Smith as he set about rebuilding in search of the success the Pittodrie faithful craved. In fact the very presence of Nicholas, who had swapped the bright lights and fast pace of London and Arsenal life to sign for the Dons, was a clarion indication of the ambitions of a club which believed it belonged at the top of Scottish football.

"When I walked into the dressing room and looked around I was impressed. As well as Willie and Alex there were the likes of Stewart McKimmie, Jim Bett, Robert Connor, Neil Simpson, Davie Dodds, Charlie Nicholas, John Hewitt – all international class players. Most of the others had turned out for Scotland at Under-21 level and were well on their way to full caps. It was a very strong group," said Smith.

But Smith was quick to put his own stamp on that Dons dressing room, launching a signing drive that marked a revolution in Scottish club football. While other teams had dabbled with foreign signings, none had embarked on the type of continental shopping spree Smith engineered. He went Dutch, quite literally, and once again Aberdeen had Alex Ferguson to thank for sowing the seeds that reaped such a rich harvest in the late 1980s and early 1990s.

He said: "I had encouraged Jim Leighton to go to Manchester United, I think he had other options to go to France, and after that had gone through Alex told me of some goalkeepers in Holland. As soon as I saw the tapes of Theo Snelders I knew he was the one. I saw tapes of him from 16, when he was playing first team football, right through to the age of 23 or 24 when he joined us. He was a giant of a man and a fantastic goalkeeper. We bought him for £270,000 and it was a great piece of business.

"I had found a market in Holland, I could see by going to games out there that there were a lot of good quality players available at very reasonable prices. Leighton had gone to Old Trafford for £450,000, Willie Falconer moved to Watford for £300,000, Peter Nicholas to Chelsea for £350,000 and Davie Dodds was sold to Rangers for £130,000. That provided funds and I knew I could buy in replacements from the continent for less.

"Willem van der Ark cost £260,000 and he was a good young player, coming to us at the right age, with a very different style from the usual Dutch player. He was so tall and strong. Hans Gillhaus was another. He had just won the European Cup with PSV Eindhoven but was out of the team and wanted to move on. Jocky went over to see him first, then the pair of us watched him. In the end it cost us £550,000 all in – the fee, the contract, the agent. He was sensational. I bought him to replace Charlie Nicholas but ended up pairing them together and both were tremendously skilful players.

"Theo ten Caat was a £260,000 buy from Groningen and I thought he would have been the best of the lot, but unfortunately I left before I saw the best of him. In the end he didn't play too many games under Willie, I don't know if he was troubled by injuries or if it just didn't work out for him. Peter van de Ven also came in. We paid £90,000 for a player who had been capped by Holland at Under-21 level and he was a superb professional. Nothing flashy, just a great player who kept things simple.

"He did a similar job to Brian Grant, who I'd sold to Aberdeen for £40,000 when I was at Stirling Albion. There was a clause in that transfer that meant Stirling actually got £20,000 more when he played a certain amount of games – I was the one who had to go to Mr Donald and ask him to pay that cheque to my old club."

But Smith's new additions were not solely overseas players. He continued to scour the lower end of the British market, in keeping with Aberdeen's proud reputation of financial prudence, and turned up the occasional gem.

"Manchester United had been looking at Paul Mason. They needed a right-back, but I'd watched him playing as a wing-back and told Alex he was too small for a defender – and that if they didn't decide to go for him in 14 days to let me know and Aberdeen would. In the end we signed him for £160,000 and that was a wonderful deal. He played all of three and a half seasons for me then another under Willie Miller before he was sold to Ipswich for £500,000.

"Others came in, the likes of Ian Cameron and David Winnie from St Mirren. Ian was desperately unfortunate because he suffered concussion after a bright start and by the time he came back eight weeks later the team was on a bit of a run and he struggled to get back in. David had been a good player for St Mirren but was one of those who didn't quite cross the bridge at Aberdeen."

In the modern-day success-starved times at Pittodrie the days when Aberdeen were still a powerful force in Scotland seem a distant memory. But they were. The Dons presented a real challenge to the millionaires of Rangers under Graeme Souness and consistently outperformed the green and white half of the Old Firm.

The Dons were no strangers to cup finals under Smith's leadership, appearing in the League Cup showdown in 1988 and 1989 and the last two of the Scottish Cup in 1990. Two of those three appearances brought success.

"I think it took me a season to get going. We lost in the Skol Cup (League Cup) Final in 1988, it was a great game but we were beaten 3-2, and finished second to Rangers in the league by six points. In the 1989/90 season we won the cup double, the Skol Cup in October and Scottish Cup the following May. We were starting to bring through the young players and it was working very well for us. At that time I would say Aberdeen was the best footballing side in the country – and that is a huge compliment to that group of players. Rangers were a really good side and spending millions.

"I always remember being asked at a press conference when I would make Aberdeen's first £1m signing – my reply was that I wasn't appointed to buy £1m players, I was employed to produce them. We did that. David Robertson went to Rangers for a fee of over £1m and, after I had left, Eoin Jess went to Coventry and Stephen Wright to Ibrox for big money. We had introduced them and brought them through and their transfers, and others like them, were the ones that kept the club in good financial shape."

Despite the cup double, only the second in the club's history, Smith was fighting a losing battle when it came to matching Ferguson in the eyes of the fans. League success would go some way to closing that gap and on a sunny day in Glasgow on 11th May 1991, his Aberdeen team came within touching distance of achieving that.

The Dons famously went to Ibrox on the last day of the 1990/91 season needing just one point to clinch the Premier League crown. It was not to be, Rangers won 2-0 and the heroic efforts of a season were to be forgotten amidst the disappointment of losing out to the club's most bitter rivals. The history books show Aberdeen finished runners-up, two points short of the Light Blues, but Smith is adamant the bare statistics do not tell the true story about the talents of the team he had moulded.

"That was a wonderful season, a fantastic run. At one point we had been nine points behind and clawed it back. I'd always wanted to be in the position to go to Ibrox on the final day of the season needing a win to take the title. On the penultimate weekend, we managed to claw back the gap even further and we needed a point for the championship.

"It's the most exciting climax to a Premier League season we had seen until Rangers and Celtic went head to head in 2003. We still had to do something that no other team had been asked to do, not even Alex Ferguson's side at the height of their powers. We had to go to Glasgow, to Ibrox Park, and beat Rangers in direct competition for the title.

"It wasn't like a cup final though. We had taken an allocation of 1,500 tickets. All credit to them, the Aberdeen fans gave it their best shot but the Rangers fans made it like a cauldron with the massive numerical advantage. On top of that, Rangers had the west coast and Central Belt support from the media. It was stacked against us, even though a lot of people had us down as league champions before that game had been played."

Ask a cross-section of Aberdeen fans about that infamous day and many will cite Smith's switch in system as a major contributing factor. Even players from that team have looked back and expressed surprise at a late change in plans which has often been blamed for the narrow miss. Smith dismisses that accusation point-blank.

"There's still a lot of rubbish spoken about us playing for a draw because we switched from 4-3-3 to 4-4-2 for the Rangers game. Manchester United play 4-4-2 every week and are never accused of being a negative team. My tactics weren't defensive. It really is rubbish to suggest that tactics were the reason for losing that game – scoring a goal was the difference. We created chances and didn't take them, Rangers took theirs."

Perhaps if Aberdeen had been able to call on Theo Snelders, who had been in inspirational form during the crucial middle section of the season, it would be a very different story. The Dutchman was missing through injury for the crunch meeting with Rangers, leaving young Michael Watt to shoulder the burden of going head to head with the imposing Mark Hateley and prolific Ally McCoist. The experience of that battle-hardened Ibrox strike-force won the day, with Watt coming in for some heavy treatment in the early stages of the match and never really recovering.

Smith refuses to look upon that one result as a blight on his team, even though many credit it as the beginning of the end of his Aberdeen career.

He added: "It was a great game and Aberdeen made the Premier League that season, it was a fantastic race. It pains me that team gets scant recognition for its achievements when people talk about Aberdeen's great years. It gets swept aside – yet nowadays two wins on the trot is an achievement. That team won cups and went so close to winning the league.

"People say I lost my position because of the result at Ibrox but that's not the case. The following season I was sitting top of the Premier League on 1st November. We lost 1-0 to Dundee United and 2-1 to Celtic and by the end of November had dropped down a place. Eventually we dropped down to fourth place and in my last game we lost 1-0 to Hibs at Pittodrie. They scored in the last minute having never been in the match."

That final match, on 23rd November 1991, marked the culmination and success of a concerted campaign by a section of the Aberdeen support to see Smith removed from his post. Demonstrations at the ground and "Smith Must Go" signs had become a feature of life at Pittodrie in the final weeks of his stewardship. That came just seven months after his side had gone to Ibrox with the Premier League prize within touching distance but the small but vocal minority had made their mind up. The manager had to be ousted.

Yet that seemed unlikely. The Dons had never sacked a manager in almost 90 years, let alone one who had brought two cups back to the north-east little over a season before.

But, as Smith discovered at the time and subsequently in his split from Dundee United, the only guarantee in football management is that one day you will be left searching for a new job. The directors bowed to pressure from the stands and Smith's contract was terminated.

His co-manager, Jocky Scott, had already left the club earlier in the season to take charge of Dunfermline and return to life as a boss in his own right. Drew Jarvie, the other piece of the coaching team, was to remain at the club until Steve Paterson's appointment in 2002.

For Smith the sacking still rankles, although he bounced back from the disappointment of Aberdeen to take charge of Clyde and then Raith Rovers before taking control at Dundee United and then Ross County prior to joining Falkirk in a coaching capacity. Time has dulled the pain of the Dons disappointment but it will never erase the memories.

The sacking of Smith epitomises the great expectations which surrounded Aberdeen in the 1980s, solely as a result of achievements by Ferguson which in hindsight were out of proportion with the club's financial clout. To this day the Dons are counting the cost of trying to live up to those aspirations after throwing money at the managers who followed Smith into the hot-seat.

He said: "It was the first time I'd been out of the top four since I'd been at Pittodrie. The first time I'd been below Celtic or below Dundee United, who were a really good team at that time. We were going to Glasgow and appearing in cup finals, beating Rangers and Celtic to win cups.

"A group of around 50 who used to drink in a bar near the ground decided they wanted me out and it became poisonous

– the board cow-towed to them. Aberdeen thought they were doing the right thing but they weren't and I told them it was a mistake at the time. I was extremely disappointed. I felt they should have supported me a bit more.

"The opposition from the fans started at a Uefa Cup tie against Copenhagen when we lost to a team who went right through to the semi-final and beat Bayern Munich 6-2 on aggregate on the way. Those fans decided that wasn't good enough for Aberdeen. Willie Miller was a messiah to them, and I can understand that because I have a tremendous amount of respect for him, they wanted Willie in charge. I had wanted to spend more time grooming Willie to take over but that wasn't allowed to happen.

"It hurt but I've still got a lot of time for the club. It's water under the bridge now but it took time to get over and I needed to get shaken out of it by one or two people."

And does Smith feel he ever threatened to emerge from the shadow of Sir Alex? No, but not for the want of trying. As he discovered, there will only ever be one Alex Ferguson in the eyes of the Pittodrie fans.

He admits: "I still feel that time in the club's history, the early 1990s, doesn't rate a mention purely because of Alex's achievements. At most other clubs what we achieved would be remembered fondly. It would be interesting to see our side against the one that won the European Cup Winners' Cup. They were different teams but I think it would be a good game – a lot of people I've spoken to say our team played more attractive football. It was certainly a pleasure to work with them."

Chapter 3

MORE THAN any championship win with Manchester United or adventure in the Champ-ions League, one trophy more than any other won by Alex Ferguson has come to symbolise his ability and style as a football manager of great repute. By leading Aberdeen to the European Cup Winners' Cup in 1983 against Real Madrid he had written the sport's own version of David and Goliath for the world to sit up and take notice of.

Now, three decades later, it is a tale you could never tire of telling. How little Aberdeen humbled the Spanish superstars with style and grace.

Best of all, it was done with a team that had cost pennies to assemble, rubbing salt into the wounds of the slain giants and appealing enormously to anyone with even a hint of romance in their body.

That most famous of Dons team was built upon a foundation of steely defensive resolve, stemming right back to the goalkeeper.

Jim Leighton may have gone on to be a Scotland star, eventually following his manager to Manchester United and England's big stage, but he cost Aberdeen not a bean.

He originally attended trials alongside Alex McLeish, John McMaster and fellow goalkeeper John Gardiner having been

43

spotted by scout John McNab. St Mirren, then led by Alex Ferguson, were also keen on Leighton, as were Morton, but the lure of a full-time contract at Pittodrie swayed him.

Leighton, who signed during the Ally MacLeod era, was allowed to continue his development on the west coast with junior side Dalry Thistle. Billy McNeill chose to farm his promising young shot stopper out to Highland League side Deveronvale, with John Gardiner and Ally MacLean also on the books and vying for a place in the reserve team as understudies to Bobby Clark.

Leighton would train at Pittodrie in the morning, work in an Aberdeen sports shop in the afternoon and turn out for Vale every weekend. He was named as the Banff club's player of the year in 1978 before earning his big break in the Dons first team after Clark had suffered a hand injury. Ferguson saw something in the young keeper he liked and decided to use him as the cornerstone for the team he was constructing.

Leighton could be classed as one of football's thinkers, studious in his approach to the game. At right back, Ferguson installed on of the game's doers. Doug Rougvie arrived at the Dons via Dunfermline United's Under-16 team, where he had won the Scottish Juvenile Cup.

He had initially been a target for Leeds United but when the Elland Road club decided their youth ranks had no vacancies, the Yorkshire side's scout Andy Young recommended the strapping teenager to his friend Jimmy Bonthrone at Pittodrie.

As a 16-year-old he was farmed out to Aberdeen junior side Rosemount by the Pittodrie club and the following term he was sent to the Highland League to step up a grade with Keith in 1973.

He won the Highland League Cup with the Aberdeenshire side before being recalled by his club. Rougvie spent two years learning his trade in the second string before establishing himself in the Dons team and became a defensive mainstay, although not in the central role most had predicted for the towering youngster. He was an imposing full-back, tall and rangy with an unshakable will to win. Just like his boss.

On the opposite side of the defence was a different type of player – but another who was free of charge. John McMaster first caught the attention of Aberdeen scout Bobby Calder while turning out for Port Glasgow Rovers, champions of the Paisley and District Under Age League, in 1971.

He shone in a Dons trial match against East Fife the following year, alongside Rovers team-mate Bobby Street, and both youngsters were signed.

McMaster, a 16-year-old left-winger, made his reserve team debut just ten days after moving to the club and the following season was loaned to Peterhead in the Highland League. He scored two goals for the Blue Toon in a 2-2 draw against the Dons in a friendly towards the end of that campaign, having also scored a double for the Buchan side in a 2-1 win against the Pittodrie reserves weeks earlier, and that form persuaded Aberdeen to recall him immediately.

After falling out of the first team picture in 1977 he attracted the interest of Ayr United but chose to stay and fight for his place, a wise decision as the champagne era began and he found himself emerging as a first choice pick under Ferguson.

While Leighton, Rougvie and McMaster had been on the scene prior to the manager's arrival, the number four in the Gothenburg team was very much a son of Ferguson.

Neale Cooper signed on schoolboy forms for Aberdeen after catching the eye with his performance for King Street in the juvenile leagues and with Hazlehead Academy. As a 15-year-old, training with Scotland's youth team, he was singled out by coach Andy Roxburgh for his enthusiasm and ability and benefited from sessions under Walter Smith and Craig Brown among others during SFA gatherings at Largs.

He went on to skipper Scotland's professional youth squad and made his debut at the age of 16 for the Dons against Kilmarnock at Pittodrie.

Ferguson had no qualms about blooding him at such a tender age and said: "Despite his youth, Neale is above reserve team football standards and with the other Aberdeen defenders playing so well at the moment, this could be the best time to promote him so that he does not suffer from lack of support as he adjusts to Premier Division football."

Cooper had to be versatile to force his way into the Dons team and his ability to slot effortlessly into a variety of positions made him vital to the squad. Midfield became his turf, having found defensive opportunities blocked by the Alex McLeish and Willie Miller pairing.

McLeish joined from juvenile side Glasgow United. Dumbarton, Hibs and a string of English sides were also keen but he accepted the challenge in the north-east and joined a growing band of west coast youngsters in the Granite City.

Manager Ally MacLeod compared the young recruit to Dons skipper Willie Young when he arrived in July 1976. He spent his first season on the Pittodrie books learning his trade with junior outfit Lewis United. McLeish used it as a springboard to success at club and international level, a key component to everything Ferguson achieved at Aberdeen.

Beside him every step of the way was his sidekick Miller. He was a 15-year-old centre-forward with Glasgow side Eastercraigs when he signed for the Dons, fresh from his juvenile outfit's triumph in the Under-16 Scottish Amateur Cup. They defeated Celtic Boys' Club 4-2 in the final, Miller grabbed a double and was denied a hat-trick by the crossbar – having scored all five goals in his side's 5-0 victory against Possil in the semi-final of the national competition.

Bristol City and Bury both took the promising Glaswegian south for trials but it was Aberdeen chief scout Bobby Calder, acting on advice from his Dons scouting colleague Jimmy Carswell, who won the race. He turned up at the Miller household with chocolates for the player's mother, cigarettes for his father and sweets for the children. Miller was recruited and travelled north during school holidays for training sessions, signing under the watchful eye of legendary manager Eddie Turnbull just a month before the coach departed for Hibs and Jimmy Bonthrone took over.

Miller had played for both the Glasgow and Scottish school select teams – as a goalkeeper for his city side at primary school age, before turning goalscorer.

After arriving on the Pittodrie playing staff he was loaned to Peterhead, hitting 22 goals as an attacker in the Highland League before his conversion to defence. It was the turning point in his career as the path opened up for a long and dis-tinguished period of service at the heart of the Dons back line.

It is only when you get to number seven on the Gothenburg team-sheet that you stumble across a player who actually cost some money – and even then, it was not Ferguson who spent it.

Gordon Strachan made his move on 23rd November 1976, the Dons parting with £40,000 and Jim Shirra to lure the Dundee captain.

Manager Billy McNeill said at the time: "This may not be the biggest signing Aberdeen have ever made but, in my opinion, it could well become the best. Gordon is only 20 years old and the club can expect at least another ten years from him. It's a great signing for the future and I'm sure the Pittodrie fans will come to realise his great ability. I have seen him on many occasions and he has seldom failed to impress me."

His wages more than quadrupled when he made the move up the A90, indicating the power Aberdeen had in the transfer market when and if it was deemed necessary to splash the cash.

Strachan's promptings from the right of midfield were deemed worthy of investing in, given the centre of the park had been taken care of in a more thrifty manner.

Neil Simpson was another free recruit. Born in London but brought up in the Aberdeenshire village of Newmachar, he began his football journey in inauspicious surroundings, turning out for the local cub pack's side as well as his school team. He went on to star for Middlefield in the Aberdeen juvenile leagues.

He caught the eye of a string of clubs as a teenager and had trials with Manchester City, Aston Villa, Sheffield United and Middlesbrough. Like so many, he opted against the bright lights of England to stay closer to home and signed for the

Dons as a 15-year-old on schoolboy forms before stepping up to the full-time staff the following year.

Scotland youth coach Andy Roxburgh was soon alerted to his potential and Simpson became a key part of the national Under-18 team before moving on to gain Under-21 honours and being capped at senior level as he continued his progress with Ferguson's dominant Aberdeen team.

Following something of a pattern, the left wing berth was one that had been considered worth pumping funds into. Peter Weir was by far the most financially significant signing in the Gothenburg team. He moved in May 1981 in a deal valued at £330,000 when the value of part-exchange player Ian Scanlon was added to the £200,000 cash payment.

It made Weir the most expensive player in the history of the Scottish league but the player took it in his stride.

Weir said: "I feel I am joining the best club in Scotland. This will be an opportunity to further my ambitions – hopefully both at club level and international level. I know I'll be in good company and want quickly to become part of the team. I'm just glad the club saw fit to buy me."

Ferguson's pursuit of his former St Mirren protege had lasted more than a year before the Buddies finally conceded the switch was inevitable.

The Pittodrie manager said: "I am delighted to secure this player. All last season he was unavailable and even now I think Saints would have preferred him to go south."

St Mirren were accused of under-pricing Weir in some sections of the media, with figures of £500,000 deemed realistic, but the Love Street club was not in a position to turn down what was still an attractive offer from Aberdeen and the deal was done. He supplied the ammunition to another man who had been procured using the carefully guarded Pittodrie cheque book. Mark McGhee was Alex Ferguson's first big-money buy at Aberdeen. He cost £70,000 when he joined from Newcastle United in March 1979 but even at that price it was a bargain.

The 21-year-old player, who had shot to prominence as leading scorer with Morton with a haul of 60 goals in just two seasons, had cost the English side £150,000 just 15 months earlier but was allowed to return to Scotland after failing to hold down a first team place.

After his first training session with his new team-mates, McGhee said: "I don't expect to walk right into the side. It is going to be a hard fight and it is up to me to play my way in. I'm happy to be an Aberdeen player. I've always regarded Aberdeen as the team most likely to break the Old Firm's stranglehold on Scottish football and I'm hoping I can do my bit in taking honours to Pittodrie."

He had been out of the Newcastle team for two months when Ferguson made his move but the wily Dons manager had seen enough of his target during his prolific Morton days to know he could cut it in the Premier Division.

Alongside McGhee in attack was a more cost-effective option, with Eric Black coming through the youth ranks to win his place in the team. Black, whose father had starred for Airdrie and Hearts, was picked up early by Aberdeen and made the journey from his Highland home in Invergordon to train regularly with the Dons from the age of 13 while playing for Alness Academy. A touch of fortune surrounded the find, with Alness teacher Ian Mackenzie writing to the Dons to suggest they take an interest in the youngster who was leading the line for his school team.

Youth coach Lenny Taylor followed up the interest and the relationship built from there, with Black signing as an S-form before becoming a professional at the age of 16. He had also trained with Highland League outfit Ross County but his first visit to Pittodrie convinced him that Aberdeen was the club for him. Billy McNeill was in charge when the initial invitation to train with the Dons was sent out but Alex Ferguson was the gaffer by the time the arrangements were put in place.

Super-sub John Hewitt, the match-winning hero from the bench in Gothenburg, had followed a similar path to his striking colleague Black. It took Alex Ferguson two attempts to land Hewitt, who was hot property as a schoolboy at Hilton Academy in Aberdeen. Ferguson tried to tempt the player to St Mirren when he was in charge at Love Street at a time when Celtic, Manchester United, Sheffield United and Middlesbrough were scouting him.

When he took over at Pittodrie, Ferguson returned to his old target and snapped up the eager 15-year-old Middlefield Boys' Club starlet in the summer of 1978 on an S-form. The Dons boss said: "He's a natural goalscorer and those are in very short supply. If the boy is prepared to work he could have a great future."

Hewitt had been a ball boy at Pittodrie as a youngster and the schoolboy international's first choice was always to join his home town team.

So there you have it – the 12 men who elevated Sir Alex Ferguson to the status that made him one of the most in-demand managers in the European game, propelling him into the limelight and giving him the platform to take his own career to the next level.

Only three of those 12 players had commanded a transfer fee when they were recruited – McGhee, Weir and Strachan – and even then the outlay was under £500,000 when combined. Good value to secure the biggest honour in the proud club's history.

The other nine had been carefully picked, cultivated and refined under the watchful eye of a manager who proved then and since that he has a priceless ability to take young players and turn them into men capable of competing with the best in the business. Who says you can't win anything with kids?

Chapter 4

LONG BEFORE the curious case of David Beckham and the flying boot, Alex Ferguson was striking fear into the hearts of grown men. While the renowned iron fist continues to dominate at Manchester United's training base at Carrington, it was in a more modest corner of Pittodrie Stadium on the north-east coast of Scotland that the man-management skills were first honed.

It was there, with his Aberdeen squad, that the now infamous hair-dryer treatment was refined as the man completed his transition to top class manager after his early groundings at East Stirling and St Mirren.

While dealing with the complex characters of players such as Wayne Rooney and Cristiano Ronaldo has become the stock in trade of a man-management master, the skills required to nurture and cajole players were evident from the early days with the Dons.

The wage packets may have been smaller and the public profiles paled into insignificance when compared to the modern generation of Red Devils megastars, but the premise was no different. As a young man, Ferguson chose to go head to head with some of Aberdeen's biggest and most revered players as he made a statement of intent early in his reign.

The highest-profile of all was a man who had the entire Pittodrie support on his side. While few dare to criticise the approach of the manager, one man has bucked that trend. Step forward Joe Harper, King of the Beach End. Harper was a hero to the Aberdeen fans when Ferguson arrived in the north-east and to this day his goalscoring feats remain unmatched.

He was also a confident character, brash and brazen...in so many ways similar to the man who he would soon find himself at loggerheads with. Ferguson blamed a poor work ethic for his failure to take the King to his heart. Harper argued he was never given a chance. In recent years literary ping-pong has seen both fire volleys at each other through the pages of their respective books.

By displaying a willingness not to let sentimentality or fan power play a part in his decision making process, the gaffer was marking himself out as a man not to be messed with. That message was sent out to the squad who saw that nobody was untouchable, to the supporters who would realise that nothing would get in the way of his pursuit of perfection and to the media who watched from the outside with intrigue and a degree of trepidation. If a player of Harper's stature held no fears, journalists had even less protection. They knew they could not step out of line.

But Ferguson was not indiscriminate when it came to picking what, in fairness, were occasional fights. While some players required the proverbial rocket, others were dealt with more sympathetically.

Right back to his very first appointment at East Stirling he laid down the law. The hard-line approach continued at St

Mirren, where he railed against a drinking culture he feared would undo his plans for the future.

At Aberdeen the control measures became more and more innovative, if that's the word for it. He prepared a pair of tackety boots with nailed-in studs as a deterrent for those who dared to think about slacking in training – winger Joe Miller was a frequent recipient, suffering the pain as well as the embarrassment of having to wear them on more than one occasion.

Trainer Teddy Scott, of his own volition but no doubt with his manager's express consent, would add an extra ten yards to the measured-out running tracks – working on the assumption the players would ease off ten yards before the finish line anyway, so that way they would be made to go the distance without even knowing it.

Then there were the mind games. Neil Simpson, a player with an appetite as legendary as his playing achievements, was tackled about his eating habits on the eve of a big game. He went out to prove his manager wrong and played a stormer. Job done.

Striker Mark McGhee reveals the terror he used to go through week on week as he waited for the team announcement. McGhee said: "Individually he was always challenging and questioning you, making you question your own ability. One of his great tricks was whenever the team was picked you were relieved to hear your name. I used to go home and say to my missus: 'God, I was so pleased I was playing' and she'd say: 'Yeah but you've played the last 36 games and scored 25 goals.' Somehow you still felt threatened."

Neale Cooper, that terrier-like midfield star, tells the story of a close encounter with Celtic's rising star Charlie

Nicholas in a top flight encounter. On the Monday before the game he had been ordered in to Ferguson's office on the Monday leading up to the match and was told: "Cooper, see that Charlie Nicholas? He is the golden boy of Celtic and the Glasgow press say he is going to slaughter you on Saturday." He threw a picture of Nicholas across the desk and ordered his young player to look at it last thing at night and first thing in the morning: "I want you ready to make sure golden boy doesn't make a fool of you or Aberdeen." The rest of the week followed a similar pattern, with Ferguson repeating the mantra: "Remember, Nicholas, golden boy, stop him!"

He did stop him. Within seconds of the kick-off Nicholas was flying through the air – unaware of the goading that had led to his unceremonious introduction to Mr Neale Cooper, of the Parish of Ferguson.

Cooper was just the type of individual Ferguson loved to work with. He was committed, he had character and he was thick-skinned.

Today, the modern breed is very different. Speaking in 2009, Ferguson said: "It's a different player character we've got today. The players are more fragile than players of 25 years ago. They are more cocooned today by their agents or the press they receive at times. They are less likely to hold their hands up and say they're at fault for things.

"If you go back 30 years ago you had a player who had a certain pride and responsibility in their own performance. They were less protected so they could come in and say: 'Hands up, it was my fault.' But today they are very protected. They are more fragile than ever. That's a lot to do with the type of people who protect them – agents.

"We had a young boy get in the England Under-21s. His agent phoned up the next day and said 'I think it's time we sat down for a new contract for the boy'. In his mind he thought that demanded a new contract. I said 'let's see how he plays for Manchester United'. But that's the way the world is now."

Back in his Pittodrie days, it wasn't agents that he had to worry about. It was the players themselves who presented the biggest man-management challenges for a rookie coach still picking his way through the minefield of club life.

Steve Archibald, a Glaswegian like Ferguson, had been signed by Billy McNeill at the start of 1978. Within months he found himself under the wing of a very different manager – McNeill, an imposing figure but gentle by nature, was gone and in his place was the new firebrand.

Ferguson would play his part in converting Archibald from a First Division midfielder to a Premier Division striker with the world at his feet. He was a league and cup winner during two years as part of the Ferguson revolution, but the pair's relationship never ran smooth. Legend has it that the manager named a chair in his office after his bolshy striker, such was the frequency of his visits to see the top man.

He also chose to go to war with club legend Joe Harper, the all-time top scorer for the Dons and not short of confidence. He and Pittodrie's new big character did not hit it off, although Harper insists he does not know what was the cause of the initial rift.

Ferguson, in his autobiography, has since levelled several accusations at the prolific striker – citing his unwillingness to graft in training as one of his complaints.

Harper, in a newspaper interview in recent years, noted: "I have no wish to speak to Sir Alex Ferguson ever again. The things he wrote in his book were the final straw. When I studied the passages that referred to me, I felt a strong desire to burn the book.

"I considered taking legal action over the contents, but how could I prove anything? It's Fergie's word against mine, and it did not surprise me that others – including Gordon Strachan and Jim Leighton – disputed other claims made in the book.

"Going by what he wrote, though, Fergie really hated me, yet I cannot recall being negative in any way when he took over at Pittodrie in 1978.

"I wish I could pinpoint the reason. All I wanted to do was to score goals, preferably for Aberdeen."

Then there was the mercurial Ian Scanlon. Aberdeen had not won the Scottish title for quarter of a century when they travelled to Easter Road on 3rd May 1980. The Dons needed a victory against struggling Hibs and for third-placed St Mirren to take a point against second-placed Celtic for the long wait to end and that afternoon in Edinburgh it all fell into place.

Steve Archibald broke the deadlock in the capital after 26 minutes and two minutes later Andy Watson doubled the advantage. After the interval a double from Scanlon, with a Mark McGhee goal sandwiched in between, put them on easy street.

With a 5-0 win in the bag, a tense wait for the delayed final whistle at Love Street ended when news filtered through the Saints had held the Parkhead men to a 0-0 draw. The Premier Division prize was Aberdeen's and Scanlon was an unlikely hero.

Unlikely for two particular reasons. The first was that he had actually quit football years earlier, claiming he had become disenchanted with the game. The second was that he had told manager Alex Ferguson he wanted to leave his club 17 months before collecting his championship medal. Fortunately, on that occasion Ferguson was in a forgiving mood and the wide man remained firmly in his plans.

Scanlon was an unpredictable talent but gave the 1980 title-winning side a valuable outlet on the left wing. His tendency to beat his marker more than once before finally delivering a cross infuriated Ferguson and provoked the famous hair-dryer treatment more than once, but Scanlon kept his place on the team-sheet.

In that championship-winning season he featured in all but seven of the league games, starting 25 games and making four appearances from the bench. He scored eight Premier Division goals, including that vital double against Hibs to clinch the flag.

Scanlon got his first big break with Notts County, joining as a teenager from East Stirling in 1972 and became a Meadow Lane favourite. At the age of 21 he topped the County scoring chart for the first time and continued to be their main man in attack until his dramatic decision to retire in November 1977, at the age of 25. He claimed to have fallen out of love with the game and planned to use an inheritance to open a pub in the Nottingham area.

His exile proved short and in March 1978 he was back in the game and back at the top after Aberdeen manager Billy McNeill negotiated a £40,000 deal with Notts County to enable Scanlon to make his comeback with the Dons.

Ferguson replaced McNeill that summer and installed Scanlon as his first-choice number 11. Just three months into the campaign he knocked on the manager's door to request a transfer after he and his wife failed to settle in the north-east. Despite that off-field unrest he still appeared in 45 games in the 1978/79 season and was back at his elegant best for the victorious league campaign the following season.

A league runners-up medal followed in 1981 before a switch to St Mirren as part of the deal which brought Peter Weir to Pittodrie. Scanlon finally realised his ambition to venture into the licensed trade when he opened a pub in Glasgow following his departure from the Buddies.

It was an era in which pubs still featured prominently in the average footballer's life, whether behind or in front of the bar. The demon drink and the lure of the party lifestyle had a part to play in one episode that could be classed as a rare man-management failure.

When Stevie Gray was unleashed on Scottish football in a League Cup tie at St Johnstone in August 1985, Alex Ferguson thought a star had been born. The Dons won 2-0, the youngster had been delivered into the top team and surely he would be around for years to come. In fact, Gray would play just 50 competitive games for the Premier Division outfit and would never fulfil the potential his legendary manager had seen in him.

Gray had signalled his ability as part of Aberdeen's team for the Scottish Youth Cup Final in 1984. His team trailed by three goals to Celtic, but the skilful midfielder delivered a sublime performance and drove his team to a 5-3 victory which included a goal to cap the occasion.

Unbeknown to the thousands who watched the rousing performance, Ferguson had taken matters into his own hands and stormed the dressing room when he should have been enjoying a night off and allowing his sidekick Willie Garner to take the team. A half-time dressing down did the trick and the kids did their club proud.

By the start of the 1985/86 season Gray, a Scotland youth cap recruited from Kilmarnock Boys' Club, was on the fringes of the first team and had been part of the League Cup-winning team as well as being capped at Scotland Under-21 level.

With incredible skill as well as decent reserves of stamina and strength, he had all the makings of a modern midfield player. Unfortunately, Gray also had some of the traits of the traditional tortured genius, with a love of the good life and trappings of his fledgling fame.

He was eventually sold to Airdrie four years after his debut and, despite helping the Diamonds to the First Division championship, struggled again to maintain focus. A spell in the Highland League with Huntly in the 1990s followed, but familiar problems with commitment became clear. Gray drifted out of football and died in 2009 at the age of 42, his talent unfulfilled.

Gray would perhaps have blossomed had he enjoyed a longer spell under Ferguson's wing. Those who did have that protracted tutelage were in no doubt about the merits of his unique man-management skills.

Doug Rougvie, that most rugged of defenders, was putty in Ferguson's hand. In relative terms, at least. He said: "A lot of players had run-ins with the new boss shortly after he arrived. He always kept you on your toes and never missed anything.

Fergie was a man-manager and knew your every step, and this scared a lot of the players. He changed the team around for certain games, which also angered them. It ended up with a lot of players visiting the gaffer's office after they had been dropped."

Even those who fell foul of his quirks somehow felt grateful for what most, in the modern game at least, would have considered to be a sledgehammer to crack a nut approach.

John Hewitt, the goalscoring hero of the European Cup Winners' Cup triumph in 1983, was not given special treatment because of his special place in Aberdeen's history.

Hewitt recalled: "Fergie's hunger to succeed was amazing, and I count myself lucky to have been given the chance to play for him.

"He was hard with us at times, some might say it was bullying. But Fergie got results and left those who played under him at Pittodrie with a host of winners' medals and happy memories. Everything I achieved in my career was down to him.

"He had a go at everyone at some stage, even in games when we thought we had done well. On one occasion we were 4-0 up at half-time and he went mental because we had made a few sloppy passes and missed chances to create a bigger lead. He wound you up so much you went out in the second half, or next game, determined to prove him wrong.

"The only time he made the wrong call was when he slated us live on TV after we beat Rangers 1-0 in the 1983 Scottish Cup Final. Fergie apologised the next day, as he knew it was harsh because the final was the week after we had won the Cup Winners' Cup, and we were all just shattered. In time, he instilled us all with the same winning mentality."

It was when matters got personal that players suffered, as Hewitt discovered when he stalled on the offer of a new Aberdeen contract. He said: "I wasn't too impressed with the terms offered to me and asked for more time to think it through. He wasn't too happy because he wanted the deal done and dusted before he went away."

Hewitt eventually signed on the dotted line, but found he had been docked £100 – for having the audacity of keeping his manager waiting. And there was another £400 still to be deducted. Fergie didn't do things by half measures.

Mind you, Hewitt knew that already. He'd once been hit in the pocket for overtaking Ferguson's car on the way back from training. His crime was, according to the manager, risking doing damage to passengers Mark McGhee and Neale Cooper.

Hewitt may not have liked his treatment, but he knew better than to disagree with the boss – if you did that, more often than not you were out on your ear. Just ask Dom Sullivan.

Reflecting on his attempt to take on Ferguson, Sullivan said: "If I had stayed on at Pittodrie, I would probably have been there for all of the successes in the 1980s.

"Fergie wanted to move me out wide on the right and play Gordon Strachan inside, as he thought I had the legs to get up and down the line. I thought I was better in the centre, as I had been a success there throughout my career – but he wanted me out wide. Looking back, I should have done what he asked. Eventually, Peter Weir was brought in to play that role."

Sullivan went on to enjoy success with Celtic, but at the back of his mind there's a twinge of regret that he chose to go head to head with Sir Alex.

It was just one chapter in an eventful time at what was an eccentric club in many ways. When asked what his most cherished memory of Aberdeen was, Ferguson told the assembled crowd at a League Managers' Association dinner: "I had a wonderful chairman there, Dick Donald. The man became like a father to me after I lost my own. I remember what he said before my last cup final with Aberdeen. 'I wouldn't mind if we lost this,' says the chairman. 'Why did you say a thing like that?!' I ask him. 'Well, I think some of these boys are getting carried away with themselves,' he says. 'Give me an example,' I say to him. 'Well, take Willie Miller, the captain. I saw his wife the other day wearing a leather coat!'"

It was the perfect grounding in so many ways. A big enough club on a big enough stage to ensure the decisions carried real consequences in terms of performance, but a small enough club to allow trial and error without fear of retribution.

Many of the skills, some subtle and others less so, were transferred to Old Trafford – including the legendary hairdryer treatment that had been honed in the home dressing room at Pittodrie. It was not uncommon for tea cups to be sent flying, perfect for honing reflexes among the assembled masses.

The propensity for firing missiles in fits of rage did not cease with the sight of the English border and it would famously come back to haunt him.

When David Beckham was left nursing a cut above his eye after being hit in the face by a flying boot, fired by his manager, it was akin to an international incident.

Ferguson was unrepentant, claiming: "If I'd tried it 100 times or a million times, it couldn't happen again – if it did,

I would carry on playing. David did not have any stitches. It was a graze. It was dealt with by the doctor no problem and we move on and that's all there is to be said about it. There's no way I could betray the trust of the players. It's 100% loyalty. It can never be anything less than that."

As Sir Alex left the news conference he was asked if he was going to apologise to Beckham, but he walked away without reply.

When Beckham published his autobiography, he revealed his fury following the incident.

Beckham wrote: "I felt like I was being bullied in public, and being backed into a corner for no reason other than spite. I went for the gaffer. I don't know if I have ever lost control like that in my life before."

Just as he had ruled with an iron rod at Pittodrie, it was business as normal following his switch to Manchester in 1986.

Gary Neville, writing in the *Daily Mail*, said: "I've heard it said that a manager can't do anything once the players have crossed the white line. Our boss has a massive effect on the team whenever a match is on. You can feel him in your head. You'll be thinking: 'Christ, I've got to go and face him at half-time. I'd better start playing better or he might rip my skull out.' He's in control. He makes or breaks your career. He decides whether you get to enjoy your Chinese meal and glass of wine with your family after a match or you sit there in miserable silence.

"It was at Anfield that I first saw what people call 'the hairdryer', although the players never referred to it as that. 'You're slipping!' the boss shouted at Peter Schmeichel. 'So are you,' the big goalie replied, just in earshot. Everyone looked up, thinking: 'Oh my God, here he comes.' And sure enough, the boss ripped Peter's head off."

Neville recalled another incident involving Ruud van Nistelrooy. He said: "We had been looking strong at the start of the following season but even in the most successful campaigns, there always seemed to be a game when it all went horribly wrong. That season it came at Maine Road in November. We lost 3-1, and the boss was steaming. You could see him looking around, ready to explode. Then Ruud walked in with a City shirt slung over his shoulder. He'd been asked to swap on the way off and hadn't thought anything of it. But the manager did. 'You don't give those shirts away. Ever. If I see anyone giving a shirt away they won't be playing for me again.'"

Neville himself endured the wrath of the boss when he made the mistake of telling him where to go, in more industrial language than that. The result was two long road trips, for matches at Fulham and Reading, without a sniff of game time. He said: "The boss had asserted his authority. I wouldn't be swearing at him again."

And there's the moral of the story – the boss is the boss. No grey areas.

Chapter 5

STUBBORN, DETERMINED, belligerent, focused, fierce, charitable, blinkered, revolutionary. He has, at times, showed signs of being all of these things in a career packed with as many contradictions as honours. What is undisputed is that displaying those qualities have brought Sir Alex Ferguson success that eclipses any of his contemporaries in world football or his illustrious forebears at Old Trafford. He has, to paraphrase Sinatra, done it his way.

Enemies have been made along the way and fights picked with the biggest organisations in the land and individuals in the game, but few have come out on top when they have gone head to head with Ferguson and been on the receiving end of his fury. Just ask the BBC, or Roy Keane, or David Beckham, or the Associated Press...or anyone who has tried to take on the master and stumbled.

I include myself in that number, after one particular abortive interview attempt in the dim and distant past that mustered little more than a string of curt one- and two-word responses to my line of questions as a rookie reporter. The subject only softened when the trump card was played and I slipped into conversation he had in fact been a team-mate of my father's – in an instant the body language switched from defence to embrace, but by then it was too late. The damage had been done and I walked away distinctly unmoved by a brief brush with football royalty.

At that stage I was a young sports reporter. Back at the office, I did not need to explain the experience I had just 'enjoyed'. Jim Dolan was the sports editor at the *Press and Journal* at that time, a man who had been there, done that and bought the T-shirt.

Dolan was himself a sports reporter for the paper throughout Fergie's Pittodrie reign, and had a number of run-ins with the sometimes irascible one, who to this day hates the tabloid term 'Furious Fergie' that was to become a byword for those who felt his wrath.

He recalls how his own exchanges with the furious one have affected his opinion of the man with the Midas touch at the helm of mighty Manchester United, even as a septuagenarian.

Dolan told me: "It was Alex Ferguson's first season at Pittodrie and he was suffering in comparison to Billy McNeill's season before. I had been told by sports editor Colin Farquharson to do a piece contrasting their fortunes and had done so, and the heading read: 'What's gone wrong with the Dons?' complete with a graph illustrating a rather wide gap in achievement.

"I had interviewed Fergie for the piece, which suggested a number of players had been dismissive of their young manager and had low regard for his abilities. The players were subsequently to be known as the 'Westhill Mafia', a nod to the commuter town some of them were based in.

"The Saturday after the story appeared saw the Dons at home and the result was another disappointment. In those early days Alex Ferguson himself sometimes dispensed the after-match drinks in the post-match press room, which doubled as his office.

"The manager asked everyone present – except myself – what they would like to drink and fulfilled their orders. As he went on about the game a very decent reporter pointed out that I did not have a drink. To which a red-faced Ferguson responded: 'If he wants a drink he can get it hissel', I'm no' serving him.'

"That retort brought roars of laughter from the assembled hacks and the same decent man who had pointed out my arid state poured a glass of whisky for me, allowing the post-game analysis to continue without further ado.

"In his final full season, when he won both domestic cups, the Dons' league form was less than impressive. They had been beaten by St Mirren at the weekend, a match at which I was not present, and were playing Clydebank at New Kilbowie in midweek.

"They lost 2-1, I think, and did not play well. I filed my copy criticising them and was astonished to hear Alex Ferguson praise his side after the game and saying what an improvement the performance had been on Saturday's.

"When Aberdeen lost a game the *Press and Journal* subeditors had a habit of using the term 'Dismal Dons' in the heading and, sure enough, there it was in the next morning's paper with an admittedly severely critical report.

"I had just taken off my jacket in the office next morning when my telephone rang. The words from the other end were torrential, beginning with: 'Aye, you, ya ....', and pointing out that Clydebank had not even managed a corner during the 90 minutes.

"When I pointed out that a defeat to Clydebank was hardly a reason for celebration, Fergie said: 'That's it. Don't you ever phone this office again, for you'll get nothing from me.' About 1pm I had heard there was a strong Dons story breaking, which meant I had to get it confirmed by the manager.

"I called Pittodrie and Alex Ferguson, still unhappy and possibly even furious, said: 'I thought I told you never to phone here again. I'm telling you nothing.' He then replaced the telephone receiver, whether furiously or not I never found out.

"I was in a dilemma. I had the bones of the story but really needed the manager's words to make it complete. I spoke to the editor of the paper to let him know why we might be the only publication in the country not to have the manager on record the next morning.

"The day wore on and suddenly it was late evening, with deadline approaching. My phone rang and it was my sports editor Colin Farquharson, who had been out on a job. Had Alex Ferguson reported me to him? Our conversations that day had been heated, to say the least. But no. Colin said: 'Get your pen out. I've got all Alex Ferguson's quotes for you. He couldn't bring himself to speak to you today, but he'll talk to you tomorrow.'

"In that moment Alex Ferguson confirmed that humanity that elevated him to another plane in my mind. It was to be confirmed when he accorded me almost VIP status years later as Manchester United manager when he saw me standing outside the ground after a testimonial match. Then he was without doubt difficult at times and full of contradictions, as he probably is now, but he showed his class after that

Clydebank defeat, though he must have done it through gritted teeth."

It would be wrong to suggest Ferguson has hardened with age. In fact the traits he displays today as the highest profile club manager in the modern game are, in fact, no different from those he displayed as a 30-something rookie making his way in the world of management. Before he had won a single trophy, Ferguson's strong will saw him locked in conflict with directors at tiny East Stirlingshire in a row over money for minibus hire. He did, at that juncture, threaten to walk away from the game altogether. Fortunately for Manchester United fans worldwide, he was persuaded otherwise.

All the while, as he cut his teeth in the management game, he was building a tandem career in the gritty world of the Glasgow pub scene. If you think a post-match grilling by the assembled media is a tough gig, try dealing with the aftermath of a gangland feud involving a shotgun. Ferguson did, all part of life at the school of hard knocks and all part of the education that served him so well on his route to the top. He had some stumbles along the way, but in general the Alex Ferguson story has been one of constant progress. That was made possible by careful planning mated with ruthless ambition.

When called upon to pass judgement in 2011 on Chelsea's bold decision to go with youth over experience with the experimental appointment of 33-year-old Andre Villas-Boas, Ferguson told the *Daily Mail*: "I was actually 32 when I started at East Stirlingshire. I was part-time with players earning about £5 a week, running two pubs in Glasgow as well. The one common denominator is that you want to be successful. I set about in determined fashion that I wasn't going to fail. I'd chosen that life. I'd been an engineer and I made up my mind that I wasn't going back to engineering. I did all my coaching badges when I was young – 23 years of age – so I'd prepared to be a manager. It's important if you want to be in the game that you prepare to do that."

Ferguson's dedication to his future trade did not go unnoticed among the instructors charged with equipping the keen student with the tools required to pursue his dream of making the big time. One of those senior figures involved in the SFA coaching courses was Jimmy Bonthrone, who was manager at Aberdeen at the time Ferguson continued his managerial studies.

Bonthrone said: "For a player to come back for extra study once they'd qualified was unprecedented. I decided to offer Alex the assistant's post at Pittodrie, but he got sent off against us playing for Falkirk for fighting with Willie Young and I changed my mind."

Those self same battling qualities would prove to be a help rather than a hindrance in the years that would follow, all stemming from his upbringing in industrial Glasgow. Indeed, he famously had a sign hanging above his desk at the old Cliff training ground proclaiming his roots in the Govan borough of his home city. That vanished with the move to the new Carrington complex in 2000, but the link will forever be in his heart.

Ferguson, in an interview with Robert Philip in *The Herald*, said: "I don't need a sign to remind me where I come from. It's etched on my heart. Reminding everyone that I was born in Govan is the one touch of vanity I have."

He rose from life in a tenement home to enjoy a millionaire's lifestyle, but he added: "I'm still the same boy from Govan I always was. Having gone on to another pinnacle in life, if you want to call it that, mixed in all manner of different social circles, acquired a knighthood and all the rest of it, none of that materially changes you. Why should it? All my boyhood mates from the Harmony Row youth club – pals I've known for over 50 years – still come down for the weekend every March to give me pelters. That's what your old friends are for; to keep your feet planted firmly on the ground. In any walk of life, it's easy to be affected by success or money but I like to think my parents would find me completely unchanged.

"They instilled in me all their traditional working-class values: discipline, good manners, honesty, decency. They also suggested simple things to keep me out of trouble like joining the Life Boys and later the Boys' Brigade. My dad was reasonably strict – not so strict that you were ever afraid of him or anything like that – but you knew there was an invisible line drawn on the lino that you shouldn't overstep.

"When he said something, he meant it but he was a very, very fair man. One of his favourite sayings was that 'if a thing's worth doing then it's worth doing well' so he was always very encouraging as regards my football. Of course, if I ever became carried away with myself then I got a clip round the ear.

"The greatest fortune in life is to be born into a loving family and my dad influenced me in every way. For example, he was a real stickler for punctuality – my mum always insisted that it was he who opened up the shipyard every morning because he was unfailingly the first to arrive for work – and it's because of him that I'm never late for anything to this day."

To this day, Ferguson speaks lovingly about his youth and particularly his football apprenticeship with Drumchapel – an amateur club fielding teams from Under-14 through to Under-18 which blooded the likes of Kenny Dalglish, Asa Hartford, Archie Gemmill, John Wark, John Robertson, Pat Crerand and Mo Johnston among others.

Douglas Smith was the man who founded the club and Ferguson has nothing but praise for a figurehead who passed away in 2004. Smith, who ran his family's successful ship-breaking business when not engrossed in his football mission, was a guiding light for the impressionable young forward.

Ferguson told *The Herald*: "Douglas Smith was a fantastic man. It helped that he was very rich but it wasn't just about money – he devoted an incredible amount of time to us. Douglas Smith didn't only teach you about football, he also instilled in you a code of life – discipline, cleanliness, good time-keeping – a trait which I'd already picked up from my dad – no swearing, good sportsmanship, but how to be competitive as well.

"He was also a great visionary. Just as Sir Matt Busby was always fascinated by European football, Douglas Smith was taking Drumchapel Amateurs to the continent in the 1950s to play in youth tournaments against Barcelona, Juventus, AC Milan, Roma, Fiorentina and Spartak Moscow. The lessons I learnt while playing for Drumchapel have stood me in good stead throughout my career – Douglas Smith was a great man and a massive influence.

"From East Stirling to Manchester United, I think if I have one quality it's that I've always been a trier. As a player I never liked losing and that has embodied my attitude ever since I first went into management. You can't win every game but if you try to win them all and show the right desire then you'll win more than you lose. And that's important as a manager because if you lose a couple of games then you can be out the door."

From Drumchapel, the young Ferguson quickly progressed. As a player he was a schoolboy, youth and amateur international as a Queen's Park starlet before joining the professionals at St Johnstone in 1960. He switched to Dunfermline four years later and in 1967 Rangers paid in excess of £60,000 to lure him back to Glasgow. The Ibrox experience was a rare disappointment in a glittering life in sport, but he went on to regroup during spells with Falkirk and Ayr United.

He had already set about gaining his coaching qualifications by that point, standing out from the crowd by his willingness to put in extra hours. The work ethic instilled from his father's shipyard background has been a huge part of his success – working around the clock to better himself and always willing to go the extra mile. Samuel Goldwyn's oft-repeated and now famous line "the harder I work, the luckier I get" clearly transfers to football as it was Ferguson's relentless pursuit of his goals that won him his first break as he impressed veteran managers with his willingness to graft at the basics to set himself on the right path.

His determination had been noted and that led to a recommendation to lowly East Stirlingshire, officially the worst team in Scotland, which in turn led to the first step on the managerial ladder at the start of the 1974/75 season.

It was an earthy environment, but even today Ferguson is adamant the parallels between the experiences of that period in his life are little different from those he encounters in the altogether more luxurious surroundings of Old Trafford.

He told *The Herald*: "There's not any difference in essence. But if you allow yourself to be affected by the star-status thing then that's when your difficulties begin. You can only achieve success when the players want to please you and not the other way around. Some people fall into the trap of trying to keep players happy all the time and allow powerful personalities in the dressing room to rule the roost but that's not management; you might as well be the assistant kit man.

"It doesn't matter whether you're managing East Stirling or Manchester United, you have to remember two things. Firstly, you've got to have them trying their utmost to win for you and, secondly, you've got to have control and discipline over them. Anything else and you're fighting against the wind.

"I've been in management for years – and every one of those years has been a learning experience but many of the principles that I brought to the job as a new recruit at East Stirling are still as important to me now at Old Trafford as they were then. In pre-season training at Firs Park, for instance, I liked to start every session with the boxes whereby six players pass the ball around while two piggies in the middle try to intercept it.

"I use it even now for a bit of fun in training but at the Shire, where the technical standard of the players was light years behind those at United, it helped improve touch and develop movement. And long, long before nutritionists became commonplace, I held strong views on what the East Stirling players ate before a game. You could see them thinking 'what the hell's this?' when they were served up grilled fish, toast and honey."

There were signs of success with the Shire, hauling them up the Second Division and boosting attendances thanks to the obvious signs of recovery. But he left with unfinished business, snapped up by St Mirren in the same league and accepting the challenge presented by a club with untapped potential. Again, he had been recommended for the role as the rookie boss made a good impression on the boardroom power brokers.

The part-time Paisley outfit had worked their way through a list of 11 managers in just ten years. It was hardly a model of stability, but the driven young coach was not deterred. He had been recommended for the post by Rangers legend Willie Waddell, manager of the Ibrox side's European Cup Winners' Cup-winning side in 1972, and had sought the advice of Jock Stein, manager of Celtic's European Cup-winning team in 1967. The big hitters were rooting for him from the start.

His approach at Love Street was radical, with Ferguson sweeping the St Mirren decks by releasing 19 players after agreeing to take the helm. Every single one of those rejected players dropped out of the senior ranks, vindicating Ferguson's judgement.

The new boss, who had laid the foundations of a youth development policy at East Stirling, set about doing the same with his new club and had quick success. He put his trust in a network of scouts and doubled the number of boys' teams associated to the Buddies, with Scottish Cup success at Under-15 and Under-16 level following soon after.

That form was replicated with the top team, with St Mirren promoted from the First Division to the Premier Division in 1977 when they won the First Division championship. They did it in style too, with an attacking style of play that won plaudits for the team and recognition for the young man in charge. Supporters responded, attendances grew and everyone was happy.

At least for a spell. In 1977, at a time when Aberdeen were sniffing around their manager, the St Mirren board handed their boss a new and improved four-year contract in a bid to nip the speculation about his future in the bud. It worked, with the Dons appointing Billy McNeill rather than Ferguson following Ally MacLeod's departure to take on the Scotland job.

Yet a year later it was all change, with Ferguson dismissed by the Saints amid a row with the board. He was 35 and unemployed, at least in a football sense. He still had commitments in the licensed trade in his native Glasgow, but that was not the career he craved.

He was not kept on the sidelines for long, with Aberdeen offering him the manager's job just days after his controversial St Mirren sacking in the summer of 1978 – taking over at Pittodrie after McNeill's defection to his spiritual home at Celtic Park. Ferguson immersed himself in his new challenge, leaving behind life in the Glasgow new town of East Kilbride and swapping it for the affluent Aberdeen suburb of Cults. His pub enterprises were shelved, football became the one and only focus.

In an interview with *The Herald*, he admitted: "I felt a measure of apprehension at taking over from Billy. Aberdeen were a successful club, they'd just finished second to Rangers in the league and only a few weeks earlier had played in the Scottish Cup Final at Hampden. On top of that, it was the first time I'd been employed as a full-time manager and it was the first time I'd be working with full-time footballers.

"What spurred me was the challenge of shaping their attitudes towards me as opposed to their attitudes towards Billy. That's when your character and determination comes into the equation. It would have been very easy just to go along with the players by simply keeping them laughing and smiling and agreeing to everything but, to me, that's the wrong way to go about things.

"The success I'd enjoyed at St Mirren also reinforced the belief that youth was the way forward. At Aberdeen the likes of Willie Miller, Alex McLeish, John McMaster and Doug Rougvie had all come through the ranks so all I did was strengthen the scouting system. I had about 16 scouts scouring the country and that was how we found Neil Simpson, Neale Cooper, Eric Black, John Hewitt, Dougie Bell, Bryan Gunn and the rest of that generation.

Aberdeen was a great environment for any lad; it was a one-team city, a great place to live for anyone with a young family, it was a close-knit community, and those were the selling points we stressed whenever we were trying to sign someone from the west of Scotland, say.

"What I had to create was a winning mentality. As great as Aberdeen is as a city, the club didn't have the kind of huge support that Rangers and Celtic enjoyed. The team was never forced over the line by the fans so maybe that's why I sometimes appeared to be on their backs; they needed a driving force and we couldn't expect the supporters to provide that. Whenever we went to Glasgow, I'd beseech them, 'Don't lose here. Don't dare lose in my city.'

"The message must have got through because they became as strong in character as they were in talent, which is why they were able to go anywhere in Europe and play in front of the most passionate crowds."

Before the football fruits began to become evident, the messy details of Ferguson's departure from Paisley were soon played out at an industrial tribunal following his claim for unfair dismissal. The young manager's practice of claiming £25 weekly expenses, which were tax-free, were at the centre of the club's case despite the admission it was sanctioned by the chairman. Disputes over bonus payments to players were also raised and Ferguson lost his claim against the club.

It emerged during the tribunal that Ferguson had agreed to take a pay cut to move to the north-east, with his salary dropping from a basic £15,000 at St Mirren to £14,000 with the Dons.

Generous bonuses were on offer if he could lead the club to success and in the fullness of time that element of the deal came into full force as the manager landed trophy after trophy, providing unprecedented value for money. Even the thrifty Aberdeen board could not grudge signing the cheques which represented yet more success for their cherished team.

As he was introduced to the press on his first day at Pittodrie, the new manager said: "Aberdeen is a fine club with excellent facilities. I know there is a good squad of players at Pittodrie but there is still a big challenge for me here. I'm a winner by nature and I want to win things for Aberdeen Football Club."

Within his first two weeks the manager was predicting a bright future; prophetically he even claimed during the 1978 pre-season that success in Europe was not beyond the realms of possibility.

Ferguson said: "What has impressed me most is the attitude of the players. Like myself, they are desperate to get started and I was very pleased to head the players who popped in for a bit of advance training and a chat speaking about going for the treble.

"That's the attitude I want at Pittodrie and I reckon that with a fair share of the breaks we will be knocking at the door. I can only repeat that I am delighted to be manager and am hungry for success.

"It's equally clear that the club directors are just as ambitious as the players. The fact that Pittodrie is Britain's first all-seated stadium is just one indication.

"I am very keen for us to have a good run in Europe for both the fans and Scottish football in general. Too often our teams topple at the first hurdle and the spectators deserve better. It is essential that we step up our game. If the players adopt the right approach and increase their game then we could do quite well."

It took five years of hard graft and careful planning, but that bold prediction did come true when the little Dons humbled Real Madrid in the European Cup Winners' Cup Final in 1983.

He had taken the helm in time for the 1978/79 season, a period in which he went from the joy of his appointment to the despair of losing his father early in 1979. In football, his team finished fourth in the league and runners-up in the League Cup but far happier days were just round the corner.

The 1979/80 season brought the league championship to Aberdeen, even though in the first two months of the campaign there was a threat that Ferguson could have been lured back to St Mirren after a boardroom reshuffle at Love Street. He was in demand, but the Dons manager was steadfast in his desire to remain at Pittodrie and guide the club to glory – the speculation about a Buddies return was killed stone dead by the manager and chairman Dick Donald.

The campaign had got off to an inauspicious start and a 3-0 defeat to Dundee United in the League Cup Final in December 1979 did little to inspire hope that the manager's optimism, in the face of some faltering performances, about the success which lay ahead was justified.

Not for the first time and not for the last, Ferguson was proved right. The Dons surged forward in the league during a season in which they beat Celtic a hat-trick of times and recorded five league and cup victories against Rangers. The old guard was changing, with the Dons pipping the Hoops to the title to become the first club outside of the Glasgow duo to win the new-look Premier Divison.

The 1980/81 term was fruitless, with Aberdeen finishing runners-up in the league just as they did the following season. In 1982 Ferguson did lift his second trophy with the reds, steering the team to the Scottish Cup in May that year. It was significant not just because it was a new prize to the boss but also because it came three months after the first real test of his commitment to the cause.

In the opening weeks of 1982 there was an approach from Wolverhampton Wanderers and Ferguson travelled to the Midlands for talks. The previous year Sheffield United had been given short shrift when they made a similar move but Wolves, who were prepared to make the Glaswegian the highest paid Scotsman in football management, were given a chance to state their case.

The outcome was swift and decisive, with Ferguson proclaiming: "I have turned them down, I'm staying at Pittodrie. There were one or two reasons but I really feel that the potential here at Aberdeen is not even half fulfilled. I believe so much in the players at Pittodrie and what they can achieve in the game. The potential is magnificent and if the players believe in themselves as much as I believe in them, there's no telling what we could do. One of the other main reasons was that the Aberdeen directors and fans have been good to me. Aberdeen is a good club to be with.

"Money does not compensate for doing the right thing – and maybe letting people down. Obviously I knew they would offer me great money, and it was great money in all aspects of it. But I don't want to talk about money as money wasn't my concern. I didn't want to let anyone down.

"Wolves are one of the best clubs in England and their tradition is unbelievable. I was pleased they came for me and the timing of their move means that I was their first choice. But I had to decide if I was doing the right thing – and I don't believe I have fulfilled my capacity as manager of Aberdeen."

Ferguson would not only have lined his pockets by moving to Molineux, he could also have cut his working hours in half. His talks with Wolves revealed that the football operation closed down at lunchtime each day, a complete contradiction to the ethic he had instilled at Pittodrie. Once the first team squad finished their work in the morning, the Dons reserves and youth players were put through their paces in an afternoon session before the coaching session turned their attention to floodlit training with schoolboy signings in the evening.

It was all part of Ferguson's vision for the development of the club and a steady stream of home-grown players were already filtering through to the first team.

His decision to stay true to the club paved the way for the unprecedented success of the 1982/83 season, with the Scottish Cup joining the European Cup Winners' Cup on a rapidly expanding managerial cv.

It also sparked what was becoming an annual battle to retain the services of their conductor for the Dons directors. The winter of 1983, as the dust settled on the Gothenburg scenes of jubilation, brought the sternest test that the board had faced in Ferguson's tenure up to that point.

John Greig had walked away from the Rangers manager's job and the Ibrox powerbrokers were casting envious eyes in the direction of the Granite City. The inevitable approach was made to a manager who had chosen to work without a contract since arriving five years previously and there was an anxious wait for everyone connected with Aberdeen.

Then, on 2nd November 1983, the *Evening Express* headline in Aberdeen screamed out "Fergie says: I'm staying". It was official, the pull of the team he watched as a boy and played for as a young professional was not enough to drag him away from his adopted home on the east coast.

Ferguson revealed: "I am with the club I want to be with. I have made the right decision, there's no doubt in my mind at all about that."

Chairman Dick Donald was at his manager's side as the landmark announcement was made, together with news of a five-year contract which would tie Ferguson to the Dons until 1988.

Donald said: "The club under Alex Ferguson's leadership can continue to progress at the highest level in Scottish and European football. We have fought long and hard to retain our outstanding manager and now it has been worthwhile. I publicly thank Mr Ferguson for his cooperation in everything we have done. What was important to us was that we wanted him to stay."

The decision was a message of intent for the Dons players too. Alex McLeish said: "If Rangers or Celtic had said they were interested in a player or manager around five or six years ago then I think it is fair to say that they would have wanted to go. There would have been no sleepless nights or any dawn pacing of the living room floor searching for a decision. They would have wanted to go.

"But that picture has been steadily changing over the last few years and I'm sure the manager's decision will be a major influence when it comes to discussing fresh contracts at the end of the season."

The five-year deal was reputed to be worth anything up to £250,000 over its duration, a far cry from the terms he joined the club on. Ferguson's stock was rising with every trophy success and he was not finished yet.

The 1983/84 season, interrupted by the interest from Rangers, ended with Aberdeen as champions once again and with the Scottish Cup resting back at Pittodrie alongside the European Super Cup.

There was no respite for the Pittodrie directors in the summer of 1984 though, with Tottenham Hotspur the latest club to pursue the man at the top.

Once again, Ferguson rejected a lucrative offer and told the Londoners to look elsewhere. He said: "Spurs made me a marvellous offer and I was impressed by their chairman, but I have been preaching loyalty to my players and have decided to stay. If I ever move, it will be for the challenge. Tottenham are capable of becoming the biggest team in English football and I'm sure they will succeed whoever they appoint – but I rejected them because I genuinely believe I am already with Britain's best."

As the 1984/85 season began it was confirmed that Ferguson had been appointed second in command to Scotland manager Jock Stein, a role which would run in tandem to his club job. He declined the assistant manager's title, preferring to be known simply as a coach to the national team.

On Hogmanay in 1984 the Dons manager's contribution to the game was recognised when he was awarded an OBE in the New Year's honours list and the celebrations continued well beyond 1st January. In May 1985 the Premier Division was won again, Ferguson completing a hat-trick of titles with the club.

He took the opportunity after seven years with the Dons to pen the first volume of his memoirs, *A Light in the North*. The book, which was written by Ferguson without the traditional aid of a ghost-writer, was an instant hit and the initial print run of 10,000 copies sold out as an adoring public clamoured to discover the secret to his success. The sales went on and on, sailing past 25,000 copies and making it a best-seller.

The start of the 1985/86 season proved tragic, with Stein's death during Scotland's match against Wales sending shockwaves throughout the game. Ferguson had viewed the legendary former Celtic boss as a father figure and was plunged into mourning at a time when he had to shoulder the burden of taking control of the national team during such a turbulent time.

He responded manfully, steadying the ship and helping to clinch qualification to the 1986 World Cup finals in Mexico where he remained in charge of Scotland. He had travelled to Mexico on the back of a successful club campaign which had brought a League Cup and Scottish Cup double for Aberdeen.

Ferguson said: "I am not using this position with the national team to promote myself into another club job or secure the Scotland appointment on a permanent basis and the Aberdeen chairman Dick Donald understands this. I'll be eternally grateful to Mr Donald for giving me the chance to try to combine the two jobs. He could easily have turned down the SFA request for my services.

"There is no way I'm going to be leaving Aberdeen at present. There is a continuity there and I'm settled there. I have been seven and a half years with the Dons and I could stay for another seven and a half years."

Ferguson was 43 when he answered the call from the SFA. He was still a young manager but there was never any question about his ability to handle the pressure on the biggest football stage of all, or his ability to juggle the commitments of club and country. In fact, his talents had even sparked attention from the continent but Inter Milan, at the tail-end of 1985, became the latest club in a long line to have the door slammed in their face when they tried to land the prize catch.

In Mexico the usual sky-high expectations of the Tartan Army were tempered, with Ferguson's team failing to make it out of the group stages, but there was still optimism at club level. For a time at least, as the end of the most fantastic era was approaching.

On 7th November 1986 a packed press conference at Old Trafford brought the announcement that Alex Ferguson was the new Manchester United manager. He claimed it was the only club in the world which would have tempted him to leave behind everything he had built in Scotland.

Ferguson, who had been appointed as a director by Aberdeen just weeks earlier, said: "It is incredible to think that a club of United's size have not won a league championship in 20 years. That is a great challenge to me. With Aberdeen I managed to break the Old Firm domination, so that has to be my aim when it comes to the teams dominating in England. It was a wrench to leave such a beautiful place as Aberdeen."

United chairman Martin Edwards had secured the services of a coach who had an incredible list of honours against his name: three league championships, the Scottish Cup four times, a League Cup, European Cup Winners' Cup and European Super Cup.

Edwards said: "I believe we have got the best possible manager for the job. Our meeting to decide who we wanted came out with a unanimous decision for Alex Ferguson. The new manager will be under the same ruling as Ron Atkinson when it comes to any further spending. We have a big staff of 20 players, which is already too many. He will have to sell before he can buy, the same as Ron Atkinson was told."

While the 1986/87 campaign ended without silverware for Aberdeen, Ferguson also toiled initially as he attempted to rebuild a crumbling giant of the English game. The well-documented dark days, when he was within a whisker of being dismissed by the Old Trafford club, were soon banished to the history books as the plan fell into place and a familiar trophy trail began.

It started with the FA Cup win in 1990, followed by the European Cup Winners' Cup in 1991 as he became the first manager to win the trophy with two different clubs. The League Cup and European Super Cup were claimed the following year and in 1993 a 26-year wait for the league championship ended. Ferguson, a hero to the Aberdeen fans, was elevated to the same status at Manchester United.

He told the jubilant Red Devils faithful: "This can be just the start for Manchester United. We have the platform, we have the resources and we definitely have the players. Now it's up to them and how hungry they are. The door is open for us. The future looks good at the moment but I won't be taking my foot off the pedal – that's not in my nature."

He stayed true to his word and the success has not dried up. The championship was retained in 1994, joined on the sideboard by the FA Cup, and the same double was won again in 1996. The league prize was defended in 1997 and then in 1998/99 the stunning treble, in dramatic fashion, of league, FA Cup and Champions League was clinched.

Since then there were another seven titles up to Manchester City's win in 2012 as well as the FA Cup in 2004 and the

League Cup on three occasions, as well as the Club World Cup in 2008/09 and a long list of Charity Shield triumphs.

For a man who was unemployed when he initially landed on the doorstep at Pittodrie, it is a remarkable list of achievements.

The longevity has been as impressive as the success, according to those who know him best. Sir Alex's son Darren, in an interview with Reuters in 2011, said: "To me, 25 years in any job, let alone being the manager of Manchester United, is a fantastic achievement. That's got to be the main achievement he's done – I know he's won all the trophies but the length of time and the amount of teams he's built is his biggest achievement no doubt."

A manager in his own right now, having been a player under his father at Old Trafford in his younger years, Darren has benefited from his dad's upbringing and traditional values himself.

His top tip for success in management? Darren revealed: "Just be honest with your players, regardless of whether it's good stuff or bad stuff or you're going to upset them. You'll get their respect if you are honest with them."

Chapter 6

IN EIGHT years as manager of Aberdeen, Alex Ferguson won the Premier Division title three times, the Scottish Cup four times, the League Cup once, the European Cup Winners' Cup and the European Super Cup. It was an impressive haul of silverware to say the least. In more than a quarter of a century since he departed, the same club has failed to break the Old Firm stranglehold on the league and has had some torturous experiences in the domestic cup competitions, save for the success in the Scottish Cup in 1991 and League Cup in the same season as well as a repeat of that League Cup success in 1995. And that's that, three trophies and none in well over 15 years since the mid 1990s. The trickle in the post-Ferguson years has turned into a fully fledged drought.

Playing devil's advocate, it is possible to draw the conclusion that the manager, the master tactician, picked his moment to leave. Certainly his successor Ian Porterfield argued, albeit to an unreceptive audience, that he had inherited a team in decline. Add to the equation the emergence of the Graeme Souness-led Rangers revolution and, after that, the Fergus McCann-backed revival at Celtic, and the picture of a changing landscape in Scottish football emerges. Without money to match the Old Firm in the transfer market, would even Ferguson have struggled to have maintained Aberdeen's form?

With the carefree, high-spending days of Old Trafford replaced by a more fiscally-aware approach to transfer dealings, it appears unlikely his Old Trafford successor will have the same pots of gold to dip into. Yes, there will be money to be spent but it will have to be spent selectively. Something which will surely influence the decision on a successor.

Is it possible for Manchester United to go on a trophy-less run in the post-Ferguson era, as Aberdeen did? Yes, all evidence points to exactly that. It may not stretch as long or wind as far, but it is not impossible. Look at Liverpool, look at Arsenal. There is nothing to guard against similar plight for United without the cajoling influence of Ferguson. If that proves to be the case, the reaction will be intriguing.

The problem does not necessarily lay in the boardroom, where the moneymen understand the potential pitfalls and limitations of their own prudent policies, but in the stands. Just as Aberdeen fans of the late 1970s and first half of the 1980s were brought up on a diet of success, so too have the Old Trafford faithful in the 1990s and into the new millennium.

In Scotland the accusation levelled at Aberdeen supporters has been one of unrealistic expectations. The fans, in response, would argue that now, after so many barren years, they are well grounded. Whereas once they would have sought to conquer Europe all over again, now they would settle for the smallest crumb of success on the domestic stage. Whatever the supporters may claim, the perception remains that Aberdeen is a club with ideas above its station because of the glory heaped upon it during Ferguson's tenure.

What has happened since then is a succession of teams wearing the red of Aberdeen – some good, some average and some poor – have been held up against the phenomenon of the Gothenburg side. Whether that is fair or not, it has been a fact of life.

Different managers have attempted different approaches to try and deal with the unique situation, most attempting to bury references to the past and to look solely at the present – as if by claiming that is what must be done, the media and the supporters would somehow choose to join the charade and ignore 1983. But the elephant in the room was always there.

One man who looked at things somewhat differently was Jimmy Calderwood. The Glaswegian, not short of confidence in any given situation, chose to embrace the spirit of 1983 and all that brought. Rather than shying away from comparisons, he reckoned his Dons players should be aiming to be held up against the greatest side ever to grace Pittodrie.

Calderwood, who took charge of the club between 2004 and 2009, said at the time: "Fergie's legacy to the Dons is outstanding and the players and managers who come here now have to deal with it. It is always going to be there and rightly so.

"The Dons had a very special side and great manager in the 1980s. To win so many domestic honours and beat Bayern Munich and Real Madrid on the way to lifting a European trophy were fabulous achievements.

"That sort of stuff should act as inspiration and make you more determined to create your own bit of history, it's certainly how I look at it.

"The game has changed so much over the last 25 years, so I know there is little chance of Aberdeen ever taking on the likes of Real in a European final again.

"We will probably never top that great night when the Dons won the cup in Gothenburg. But we should be able to get Aberdeen up to the level where we are one of the main competitors for domestic honours.

"That is our aim and it is a realistic one. Create your own history."

Calderwood did not win any honours with Aberdeen, like so many of his predecessors. What he did do was restore respectability with a string of top-half finishes and bring European football back to Pittodrie as a result.

The European nights more than anything served to bring the memories flooding back, not least when the Dons were drawn to play Bayern Munich in the Uefa Cup in 2007/08. Pittodrie was rocking, swaying with anticipation. It was the type of red hot atmosphere that made it a privilege to be in the ground and experience the occasion, a hint at what 1983 was all about for those who were too young to sample it at the time.

The players responded to the promptings from the stands, earning a 2-2 draw in the first leg at Pittodrie in a pulsating match that captured the imagination of the current crop of supporters. Okay, so Bayern won 5-1 on their own soil to book a place in the next round, but that's not the point. The hammering in Germany did not negate completely the feel-good factor from the initial result. Bayern had, quite famously, been one of the big names dispatched during the run to the final in 1983 – Calderwood's side had fallen short of doing that.

He remained philosophical, adding: "You cannot compare that era with the game in 2008. It is well nigh impossible to achieve what Sir Alex did here as he competed on a level par with the Old Firm and Dundee United, but to beat Bayern Munich and Real Madrid, the biggest club in the world at that time, was incredible.

"The expectation levels are still here among the supporters to an extent and it is part and parcel of being at this club. People are realistic but if we lose three games in a row it is panic time here and I accept that. We haven't been that far off third place in every season I have been here and I take a lot of pride in that."

Calderwood, whose side tackled Manchester United in the 2008 testimonial match for the Gothenburg Greats, is a Govan boy – just like Sir Alex. Like every Scottish manager, he takes inspiration from the achievements of the star among their number.

He added: "Sir Alex is in at 6.30am every morning and he sees everything at the training ground at Carrington. His office overlooks the whole complex and he doesn't miss a thing.

"It says a lot about the man that he is bringing his team of superstars here for his former players but I also view it as a reward of sorts for my players for their efforts last season."

Calderwood's assertion that the past should motivate rather than intimidate his players is one that is supported by Ferguson himself.

Well aware of his legacy at Aberdeen, Ferguson appreciates that his achievements have impacted upon each of his successors in some shape or form.

Speaking in 1999, the year he made Manchester United kings of Europe to ensure whoever succeeds him at Old

Trafford will face shouldering a similar burden, he said: "It doesn't matter where you manage, everywhere is a challenge.

"For instance, when I went to Manchester United I was delighted with the tradition at Old Trafford because it was great to follow someone like Sir Matt Busby.

"Maybe the problem at Aberdeen is that people come here and worry about what Alex Ferguson has achieved and that is not the way it should happen.

"Anyone coming in should be proud of what Aberdeen has achieved not just under Alex Ferguson, but over a long period. The club has a good tradition. The past should motivate people and not put fear into them.

"A lot of the pressure is coming from the fans because the club won the European Cup Winners' Cup and a lot of the fans still think they can do that, but they are not as realistic as the people actually in the game. They are fanatics and they live their life in optimism."

In the good old days, money was not the decisive factor when it came to domestic honours. While Rangers and Celtic had traditionally dominated, a club like Aberdeen – thanks in no small part to the prudence and good business sense of chairman Richard Donald – could compete to sign the same players and subsequently could match the big two on the pitch.

A huge gulf has developed since then, but the basics remain the same. Ferguson added: "My goals were straightforward when I joined Aberdeen – to beat Celtic and Rangers.

"The first hurdle is not to worry about the past, but to win anything in Scotland you have got to beat the Old Firm and it is not going to change."

Roy Aitken's class of 1995 demonstrated that philosophy. A former Celtic captain himself, Aitken was far from scared by the prospect of going head to head with his former club and his team defeated the Hoops in the semi-final of the League Cup before going on to win the prize by beating Dundee in the final.

Duncan Shearer was a goalscoring hero in the 2-0 win in the final, along with Billy Dodds. Shearer cannot believe he is among the last group to have claimed a winner's medal as an Aberdeen player, but knows how difficult it is for the management teams to achieve success.

He has a unique perspective, having served with distinction as a player as well as having worked as a coach at Pittodrie during his time as assistant manager under Steve Paterson between 2002 and 2004.

Shearer, now on the coaching staff at Inverness Caledonian Thistle in the SPL, told me: "Aberdeen is a club which should at least be reaching cup finals on a regular basis, I don't think that is an unrealistic expectation.

"I certainly never expected for a moment that, almost 20 years on, we would be talking about our trophy win being the last one. People can say what they like about Hearts or about Hibs, but to me the third biggest team in Scotland is Aberdeen and always will be. The history of the club has a lot to do with that, so does the fan base. The supporters deserve success, they give their team wonderful backing.

"At Caley Thistle, we lost Johnny Hayes to Aberdeen because they could pay him far more than we could at Inverness. So it is not a level playing field for the teams outside of the Old Firm – Aberdeen, I would think, have the third biggest playing budget in the SPL and should be aiming to compete at the right end of the table and to be reaching the latter stages of the cups. But it does not always work that way – even having the biggest budget, never mind the third biggest, is no guarantee for success. The money has to be spent in the right way if cup finals are to become a regular event again.

"Recreating what happened in the 1980s is a different story altogether, for several reasons. For one, all of the success came under the best manager in the world in Alex Ferguson. The importance of his role cannot be underestimated.

"For another, Rangers and Celtic were strong at that time but in the years that followed they went on to overtake the rest of Scottish football completely. They moved into a mini-league on their own and that is shown by the fact nobody outwith the Old Firm has ever won the SPL.

"The financial gulf was nowhere near as big and if Ferguson wanted to go out and buy a big-money player he had the freedom to do that. Its just that he didn't feel the need to that often.

"I would say it is definitely a lot more difficult now for a club to compete with Celtic, as champions, than it would have been at that time. Would Alex Ferguson achieve half of what he did in the 1980s if he were to come back and take charge of Aberdeen now? Logically you'd have to say no, but you just never know."

Shearer became an Aberdeen player in 1992 when he was signed by Willie Miller from Blackburn Rovers, well after the glory of Gothenburg in 1983.

He could, however, have been part of the Ferguson era had things worked out differently for him. As a promising young Highland League player, he travelled south for trials with

Aberdeen and impressed in his first stint. Failure to return for a second trial spell put paid to the prospect of a permanent switch and he ended up at Chelsea instead, the first stop on a winding route that eventually brought him back to Pittodrie.

The stint at the club in the early 1980s allowed Shearer to work with Ferguson and Archie Knox, witness the stranglehold they had on everything that went on at the club. He was impressed by their attention to detail and their demand for high standards, little realising that one day the boot would be on the other foot and he would be leading the Dons in their training sessions.

It also allowed him to see at first hand the quality at Ferguson's disposal during the trophy-laden glory years.

Shearer added: "He had a great group of young players to call upon at Aberdeen, supplemented by some very shrewd signings. At Manchester United, when the success began to flow, he had a great group of young players to call upon at Old Trafford, supplemented by some very shrewd signings.

"It is no coincidence that both clubs have followed similar paths under Ferguson. The young players do not just appear by chance – it is obviously an area he chose to look at early on in his time at Aberdeen and again when he had moved to Manchester United. If you get that right, eventually the results will follow."

As boss of Caley Thistle's Under-20 team, Shearer knows better than most the importance provincial clubs are placing on rearing their own players. It is the only way forward for teams in Scotland as the financial belt continues to tighten.

When he returned to Pittodrie as assistant manager to Steve Paterson in 2002, the duo were tasked not only with putting a winning team back on the park but also with slashing a wage budget which had spiralled under Ebbe Skovdahl.

Paterson's personal problems ended their mission prematurely, but Shearer believes supporters had already begun to lower their sights to stay in tune with the financial situation at the club.

He said: "I don't think expectations among the fans are too high. Every supporter wants to see their team win things, but I've never been aware of the Aberdeen crowd believing they have a right to win.

"The expectation doesn't stem from the stands, it comes more from looking around the club and realising how successful it once was. How many fantastic players have pulled on the shirt. That can put you under a certain type of pressure.

"I thrived on that – I used to listen to the stories about trophies being paraded through the town, about the streets being lined all the way in from the airport to the city centre, and wish I could have been part of that. I thought that if I worked hard then maybe we could bring that type of experience back to Aberdeen. It was inspiring to think about everything Alex Ferguson's team had done.

"There were players who wilted in the face of that, there's no doubt. Some perhaps didn't realise how big a club it was until they arrived and started to appreciate the history and the achievements of the past. They were knocked off their stride by that and couldn't impose themselves. It takes a certain type of character to handle playing for a big club – and Aberdeen is a big club."

Since Shearer's time as assistant manager, a succession of men have attempted to lead the club to domestic success.

set the ball rolling he dismantled the team he had inherited from Alex Smith at Aberdeen when he took over in 1992 and tripped as he ran before he walked.

The Miller experience is perhaps a lesson from the past that translates to the future. With the likes of Neville, Ryan Giggs and even the quiet man Paul Scholes tipped as potential managers of the future, it seems unlikely but not impossible that the Old Trafford regime will be brave enough to promote from within and plump for a rookie. Miller found to his cost that going from playing legend to managerial incumbent is no small task; a job that's been made to look effortless by the godfather of management isn't perhaps as simple as it may appear.

His fellow Dons team-mate from the glory days of the 1980s, Mark McGhee, found the going no easier when he had a shot at what has been described as the impossible task of trying to in some way emulate Sir Alex's achievements. McGhee had his go in 2009/10 but ran into the same problems as so many other pretenders to the throne. Expectation simply does not match realistic aims for mere mortals, but it won't stop people from trying and particularly people who have been touched by the style of the man they are all so desperate to follow.

What is clear is that the manager leaves an indelible mark – and the occasional scar, in the case of David Beckham – on all those who play under him. Look at virtually every league in Britain and there will be a Fergie legacy in some shape or form, from Mark Hughes at Queens Park Rangers to his son Darren in the Championship with Peterborough, Neale Cooper's Hartlepool in League 1 or Mark McGhee's Bristol Rovers in League 2. From George Adams, his first ever signing as a manager, now leading Ross County as director of football in the Scottish Premier League, so the list goes on.

Is it possible that the Sir Alex connection has helped give some would-be managers a leg-up in the most cut-throat of businesses? The sheer weight of numbers of those who have flown from under his wing to stand on their own two feet suggests that may well be the case.

Of the former Ferguson proteges from the Aberdeen era, Gordon Strachan has had more success than most. His achievements with Celtic in particular, when he led the Hoops in dominating the domestic scene, make him the standout man. Neil Simpson, a former team-mate of Strachan at the Dons, said: "There's no doubt that working under Sir Alex at an early age has helped to give Gordon and others a real grounding. The players that featured in Gothenburg all have real drive and determination.

"I suppose having had Sir Alex as a boss early in their careers made a big difference. Just being part of a winning team and seeing the way Fergie worked has stood us all in good stead."

Alex McLeish went on to big things too, leading Rangers to trophy after trophy before taking on the challenge of leading Scotland. Success in England with Birmingham City in the League Cup followed, and former Dons defensive partner Willie Miller believes Ferguson's stamp has been on all of his old team-mate's victories.

Miller said: "We had a positive club in Aberdeen. We hit a very special time in the history of Aberdeen in the 1980s.

"There were a lot of young players who came into the club and were given the opportunity by Sir Alex Ferguson, who was probably the most positive thinker ever. But he had guys with a like-minded attitude in the dressing room and you see these guys sprinkled throughout football. McGhee, Strachan and McLeish, even my small part at Aberdeen, Eric Black as well.

"Sir Alex was the master of making people believe and I'm sure Alex McLeish has taken that from him and is using that."

What each and every one of them knows is that they have the support of their one-time boss – and that his all-seeing eye is watching their every move.

Eric Black parted company on bad terms when he left Aberdeen to join French side Metz in 1986. The move left a sour taste in the mouth of Ferguson, who jettisoned the striker from his Scottish Cup Final team when he got wind of the plans.

Yet, when Black was appointed as manager of Motherwell in 2001, one of the first cards to land on his desk among those wishing good luck was one from the top office at Old Trafford. The message inside read: "Welcome to the rat's world."

Black did indeed find it to be just that, and opted to settle back into life as an assistant – having served alongside, most notably, Steve Bruce at Birmingham City, Wigan Athletic and Sunderland.

There is no doubting the influence his Aberdeen days had on him, including the legendary status that accompanied his goal against Real Madrid in the 1983 European Cup Winners' Cup Final.

He said: "On the night we knew we had achieved something pretty special, but it was only later when you look back at it that you think how big the achievement was because at the time we were on such a roll and there was such an expectancy to keep winning that we were probably spoilt.

"We had six years from 1980 to 1986 and if it wasn't a title then it was all the cup finals and it just seemed to go on and on.

"We were in the groove and I suppose a lot of credit has to go to Archie Knox and Alex's man-management.

"I can see he [Ferguson] set such standards with us and himself that he continually puts you under pressure to achieve because otherwise you fail. I can understand his thinking at the time was once Everest was climbed he was looking for a bigger one." Then came the fall-out, and the two men went their separate ways.

Looking back at his good luck card at Motherwell, Black can't help but chuckle. He said: "Classic Fergie. There had been no real contact with him for the best part of 15 years and then he sent me a card wishing me all the best.

"I thought it was great though and every time I've met him down here since he couldn't have been better. I think you are always an individual, but coming through a certain management system undoubtedly leaves traces and gives you parameters and standards.

"We've all undoubtedly taken things from him, I don't think there's any doubt about that. He has his faults, but what you can't do is criticise what he achieved and how he achieved it because he's probably the best ever."

Black has been linked with the Aberdeen job at various junctures in his own career, but has yet to take on that particular challenge.

His one-time strike partner McGhee did, and is no doubt still nursing the bruises after a torrid time at Pittodrie in which everything that could have gone wrong did.

CHAPTER 7

When he arrived in 2009, McGhee was greeted by these words of wisdom from his former coach Archie Knox: "Aberdeen fans cannot expect Mark to come in and work miracles overnight just because he was part of the Cup Winners' Cup-winning team in 1983. Forget Gothenburg, that was 26 years ago.

"It is in the past, and Mark was appointed manager because of his managerial skills, not because of his history at Pittodrie. He is a respected manager with a strong track record, but the fans cannot expect too much straight away.

"Aberdeen – and Scottish football – are very different now than they were in the 1980s. Mark will not have a lot of money to spend. Ultimately, what Mark achieves will come down to the tools he will be given to work with at Pittodrie.

"If he is not given that much scope to take in the players he wants due to funds, it will be difficult. Mark is thought of very highly in the game and is both technically and tactically very good."

Those qualities counted for very little during a period in which McGhee's signings simply did not do their job. Legendary status could not protect him, and he left damaged by the experience of trying to recreate the good times. He went away, regrouped and came back with Bristol Rovers – it seems the will to succeed never leaves the Ferguson proteges.

That staying power is something that must give their mentor a sense of pride. He keeps tabs on each and every one of them, always on hand to lend advice when called upon.

He classes one of his most important legacies as the number of future managers he has helped to nurture.

In an interview with the *Evening Express* in Aberdeen he said: "One of the greatest things for me is that so many of the Aberdeen team that won the Cup Winners' Cup have stayed in the game in different capacities.

"During their careers they were all terrific players, but have gained something by being at Aberdeen. I'm really proud that these men have made it into management. Somewhere along the line I have helped them to learn something.

"When a football team stays together as long as the one I had at Aberdeen at that time did, then people tend to evolve together. I was there for eight years, but the team that transformed the history of the club was born before Gothenburg. That was a golden time for the club – you just hope that they take things away from that.

"It looks as though they have, and all of the lads had, and probably still have, that great competitive edge. As individuals they wanted to win, but as they grew as a team they formed different relationships.

"I still speak to big Alex McLeish, Willie Miller and Neale Cooper regularly. I see some of them quite often and it's always great to catch up with them – you can tell that their period at Aberdeen has been very influential on their careers."

That opinion is seconded by George Adams, the man who was Sir Alex's first signing as a manager at East Stirling and who was later reunited at Aberdeen where Adams became a youth coach under Ferguson. Since then, Adams has established himself as a a star-spotter extraordinaire with first the Dons, then Celtic, Motherwell, Rangers and as director of football at Ross County during the Highland club's rise to the SPL.

Finding the right coaches to nurture the right young players has been a vital ingredient of the Adams success story and he has often returned to Aberdeen FPs.

He explained: "Alex Ferguson taught great habits. The Fergie factor, or whatever you like to call it, made sure any youngsters who went to Aberdeen in the 1980s got a great grounding.

"They were taught the importance of discipline and need to be willing to work hard to get on in the game. Fergie also made sure his senior players followed those same values and allied that with a real will to win. That is why so many of his former Aberdeen players have been able to stay in the game as coaches and managers."

On occasion, the influence has been double strength. Two former scholars at the Ferguson college of football – Eric Black and Steve Bruce – went on to forge a bond together, perhaps formed on the back of mutual understanding of the tribulations they went through under their legendary boss at Aberdeen and Manchester United respectively.

The duo worked together at Birmingham, at Wigan and at Sunderland and established an excellent understanding.

They are different animals – Bruce had been the stalwart centre-half who barely missed a game, credited for playing through the pain barrier to steer United to success after success. He is one of Ferguson's prize pupils, a Grade A student.

Black was more of a rebel, courtesy of his decision to jump ship and sample the French game with Metz. By the age of 28 the striker was washed up, a back injury forcing him out of the game. He regrouped, returned to Scotland to qualify for his coaching badges and worked with the Scotland Under-18 and Under-21 teams during Craig Brown's tenure as national team boss. Black's path took him to Celtic, where he worked under Wim Jansen, Jo Venglos and John Barnes, before he stepped out on his own at Motherwell. Coventry City was added to his cv before he teamed up with Bruce.

He said: "Each manager had his own style, ways and ideas. Each was different and I learned something from all of them."

Black and Bruce eventually went their own way in 2012, on the back of their departure from Sunderland. Bruce wound up in charge at Hull, Black as assistant to besieged Steve Kean at Blackburn Rovers.

The Scot said: "I had worked with Steve Bruce for eight years but I am here now and have given my commitment to Steve Kean. I am happy here, I want to work here and I want to be successful here. I am really excited about the project that Steve Kean has outlined.

"We are so media-led now and the perception of supporters and the media in terms of expectation. The hardest thing for a manager now is to manage the expectation of the supporters or the owners. That is a hard, hard challenge. It is managing up the way and out of the way rather than just those close-knit players you have round about.

"I think Steve has shown phenomenal and incredible dignity to have taken the pressure and to have worked on his beliefs and philosophies and continued to work with the players on a day to day basis. I think he deserves a lot of credit. Now the supporters can see that and are recognising the work he is putting in and I hope that can continue.

"I enjoyed every minute with Steve Bruce but you do probably drift into a comfort zone. You get caught in that and this will freshen me up as an individual and coach and hopefully I can bring some ideas to the party."

Inevitably, conversation at Black's unveiling at Ewood Park turned to his former Dons boss. Time has not mellowed the memories.

Black said: "At the time I can't say I particularly enjoyed playing under him. I enjoyed winning all the things we did but I was more terrified of him, and probably remain a little bit like that to this day. But I think it is only when you go into management you realise how good he is. As a player it is a totally different perspective. Once you go onto the management side, I could see the reasoning behind what he did.

"Without any doubt any player who passed through his hands would have been marked in some way in terms of the discipline and their ambition. It is only now, I am on this side, I am starting to reap the benefits."

Both he and Bruce had benefited, particularly during the tough final season at Sunderland when the supporters began to turn against them and the going got tough. When that happens, the tough get to work – and Sir Alex was right at the front of the queue to gee up his former players.

Bruce revealed: "I've been very fortunate like that. He said: 'Are you OK? It's been a bit tough, but don't stop believing. Make sure your body language doesn't change – stick that fat chest of yours out and get on with your job.' I was there in the early days when it was really difficult [for Ferguson]. But I probably saw him at his best – striving to turn around Man United.

"I go back to a night when we were bullied and beaten by Wimbledon. After that, Sir Alex decided to bring in the right type of people to represent the club, to represent him. There were arguments, fights, all sorts, but look at that spine – Schmeichel, Ince, Hughes, Robson, Cantona, people like that. Unbelievable."

Bruce has never scaled the managerial heights that perhaps many at Old Trafford would have hoped, or expected. Ferguson is in that number, and he retains a soft spot for his former skipper and was clearly hurt by his treatment at the hands of the Sunderland fans. He publicly pleaded for patience and lambasted the Black Cats supporters who turned on their manager. It was to no avail.

The appreciation is mutual. Bruce has made it clear he believes that with Ferguson in charge, any of the rivals for the crown would have enjoyed success. Indeed, he claimed: "He is a genius. He is the greatest ever. I don't think anyone will get close to his achievements."

Bruce was a grizzled competitor, never knowing when he was beaten and refusing to give in to injuries and niggles even as age began to catch up with him. He also had the guts to cut it as a Ferguson player.

He said: "If you couldn't stand up to him and his demands, and many a player couldn't, then you couldn't play for Man United. That was his mentality, to have people around him who were born winners, like he was. He wanted people to respond to it and react to it rather than shrink from it.

"He would just shout right in your face. We all answered him back, but there was only ever one winner – him, and rightly so. For all of us who had it, you just accepted it. It made you better and it made you stronger. In the early days, we knew it was coming because Archie Knox had a way of telling us when we were going up the tunnel. He'd tap you on the shoulder and tell you to get ready, it's coming.

"The great thing about it is that once it was done, it was done. On the Monday it was back to normal, he never held it against you. Just make sure you were better next week."

Bruce, with a rub of the green and results falling his way, could have served his managerial apprenticeship and worked his way through the ranks to be knocking on the Old Trafford manager's door by now, ready to take over from his former gaffer. It didn't work that way for him, instead he has found himself slipping further away from that dream opportunity and having to make way for younger, fresher alternatives.

His one-time defensive colleague Gary Neville is perhaps the fastest rising star. When he retired from playing, the experienced full-back was earmarked for a coaching role immediately at Old Trafford. Ferguson said at the time: "I do think he has a role to play as a coach, I really do, particularly with the young players. Gary has been a great example to the young players in the professional side of it. But on the other side, the Academy, we should have that presence and coaching ability Gary has. He is taking his badges. He is ready to go into coaching and we will just find a role for him.

"He is a fantastic, incredible man. He came to us as a 13-year-old boy, an avid United fan. He has been that way all his life. He has made a great career out of a fantastic will and determination to be the best. He is an absolute legend at our club and will remain so for the rest of his life."

When Neville's legwork paid off with his promotion to the England set-up under new boss Roy Hodgson in 2012, it was with his mentor's blessing.

Neville revealed: "Even before I went to my meeting with Roy I knew that it was something I wanted to do and after that I went to see Sir Alex. I had already made my mind up but I wanted him to be one of the first people to know about it. I was panicking, as you do walking into his office, but he had known about it ten days before me...as per usual. Roy had spoken to him. That is just typical. He thought the role Roy was speaking about would be very good for me, he was positive.

"You don't sit down when you're five or six or 37 and say: 'I'm going to be England coach in six months' time', you get invited. It felt like a special moment in my life. I don't get emotional, I've never cried at a football match, I've never been somebody who gets too overboard or too down, I just keep pretty level but I knew it was something important."

That was a far cry from Neville's emergence among a crop of young players in the 1995/96 season. The memories linger long for the England man, lessons he has taken with him to his new role on the international stage.

He said: "He told us that if we were good enough we would always get the chance and he stood by that. We joined in 1992 and you never think one of you can come through, let alone six or seven of you coming through and playing in the same first team for ten years together. That will be one of the focal points of his legacy: bringing that 1992 team through and winning the European Cup with them seven years later.

"The real starter for us was the first day of 1995/96 when he put six or seven of us in and that first day at Aston Villa and said 'look, away you go lads. This is it'. We had a bad start, but then we won three games in the next seven days after that and we just felt unbeatable.

"We'd always won trophies as young players, every trophy we could, so this was the next progression for us. We'd never not won. In our first year together as a team we won the double, and he knew it was coming. He saw it coming before everyone else, he had faith in us and we delivered for him.

"To be at the club for so long is staggering. You would never believe that it could happen. Manchester United had Sir Matt Busby, so to have someone who has replicated his longevity at the club and surpassed his success, you would never believe it could be achieved. That's the magnitude of what Sir Alex Ferguson has done for the club, and more than that: the success, the way he's played, bringing through young players and the performance levels over that time. Everything has been right.

"It's not just one team that he's inherited or bought. He's had to change it and move with the times. You're probably talking about five teams he's built over 25 years to achieve this success. A manager struggles to build one team, but for one manager to build five successful teams at this club is unbelievable."

And what will be the Ferguson legacy? According to the man who is among those tipped as a potential successor, there will be many. Neville said: "Longevity and success. The type of football he's played, the young players he's brought through, so many things. But mainly the success. To be honest, Manchester United is the football club and it has to win trophies, has to achieve things and that's what he's done. He's lifted more trophies for this club than any other manager in its history and that will be his legacy."

Chapter 8

TODAY THE question is which of the Manchester United players, present or in the near past, could be cut out to lead one of the biggest clubs in the world? Gary Neville has been mentioned, so too has Ryan Giggs. Both have demonstrated the mentality to cope with life at the very top during sterling service at Old Trafford. But nobody can guarantee that playing accomplishments will translate to success in the dugout. Lady luck has a part to play – just ask Sir Alex.

As a player he had hit the peak when he walked through the front door at Ibrox to join the pantheon of Rangers greats. He was a big signing and had arrived at a big club with ambitions of dominance not only on the domestic stage but in Europe too, having reached the final of the European Cup Winners' Cup in 1967 only to fall at that last hurdle. Having arrived on a euphoric high, the realisation that the big-time dream had come to a crashing end was a cruel blow for an individual fuelled by the fire of ambition.

It was during a summer Scandinavian tour that Ferguson was hit with the news that his Rangers career had ended, he was being shipped out. Manager Davie White informed him of his decision and Ferguson retired to the team hotel to mull over his next move, before drowning his sorrows with team-mates who were there to help pick up the pieces of a playing career that was in danger of crumbling.

Among those team-mates was my own father, Dave Smith. As Ferguson recalls in a throwaway line in his autobiography, the two of them headed for a Copenhagen nightclub to put the world to rights and erase the pain of the day's events. That little line in *Managing My Life* begs the question: two men, two friends and a crossroads. While Ferguson's path was heading away from Ibrox, my own father's route was travelled with Rangers in the years ahead and led to Barcelona, as part of the European Cup Winners' Cup-winning team of 1972. The ambition had been realised, but Fergie was not part of it.

As his former team-mates were defeating Moscow Dynamo 3-2 to lift the silverware, Ferguson was winding down his playing career with Falkirk and Ayr. He has expressed in detail his disappointment about the circumstances of his departure from Rangers in more recent years – knowing he could have been part of that momentous continental win had it not been for the decision to cut him loose must have hurt. He had set out in football to scale the heights and had watched while his friends and former colleagues had become legends.

There are two options at that point: descend into bitterness or come out fighting. Not surprisingly, he opted for the latter. When the 1972 team gathered in Glasgow to mark the 40th anniversary of their triumph in 2012, the man chosen to speak to the hundreds gathered for the celebratory dinner was none other than Rangers FP Alex Ferguson. Illness forced a late call-off on the night by the VIP guest, but the presence of his name on the bill for the evening lent itself to reflection.

Of all the men deemed superior in a playing sense in the late 1960s and early 1970s by Rangers, no-one has ever come close to matching his managerial achievements in the years since. On the playing side, however, they did. My father was crowned Scotland's Player of the Year in the same season the European prize was clinched and his name was joined on that particular roll of honour by 1972 skipper John Greig, stalwart Sandy Jardine and striker Derek Johnstone. An achievement that Ferguson, at his playing peak, would undoubtedly have walked over hot coals for.

Five sampled management, at various levels and with varying degrees of success. Again, my dad was one of them, Greig was another, so too did Johnstone and Tommy McLean and Alex MacDonald. None would scale the same heights. The big question is why? Decisions, decisions, decisions – that's the simple answer.

As my father explained to me, Ferguson developed the ability to put himself in the right place at the right time. He said: "I think anyone who says Alex was marked out for greatness as a manager from a young age is exaggerating. In truth, I don't think you can tell which player is going to turn out to be a successful manager – not least because luck plays such a huge part.

"Of the team of that era, I would imagine most on the outside would have predicted John Greig, as the captain, would have been most likely to have a long career ahead of him in coaching. It didn't pan out that way.

"The truth of the matter is that every person in that dressing room would, at one point or another, have looked upon coaching and management as a logical next step. We were not part of a generation who could retire off the back of the living we had made as players, so staying in the game in some shape or form was a necessity as much as an ambition. That worked out differently for each and every one of us – none could have predicted the type of success that Alex would go on to have."

The fact he had an early start to life in the coaching profession owes as much to gut instinct as anything Ferguson has achieved since the 1970s, and there has been plenty. He made a judgement call when it came to leaving Rangers and that one simple decision was to colour his life from then on in.

My dad said: "On the day Alex left Ibrox for the last time, I went with him to the train station. He told me he was ready to sign for Nottingham Forest, but was going to return a call from Willie Cunningham, who was manager of Falkirk at the time, out of courtesy. He ended up changing his mind, and signed for Falkirk rather than Forest and he was given the chance to start coaching, which in turn led to the East Stirling manager's job. If he hadn't had that change of heart, if he had gone and played in England, his life would have taken a completely different course.

"Football is no different from any walk of life, in that it is all about making the right choice at the right time. As with every decision, if you are successful then you have made the right choice – but whether that is down to good fortune or something more than that, nobody can ever tell. How much is luck and how much is down to judgement?

"He was a Rangers fan and had been given the chance to live the dream by playing for 'his' team. To be told he was no longer wanted was hard to take, particularly because it was through no real fault of his own. His face didn't fit, and that was that – but he didn't fail at Rangers through lack of effort on his part.

"He gave his all every time he set foot on the training pitch or ran out in a game, that was the type of character he was. He's exactly the same as a manager and age hasn't changed that. He is as enthusiastic about football today as he was in his 20s.

"For anyone who has played for Rangers, leaving is a huge wrench. There are very few who have moved on to bigger and better things, generally you will be taking a huge backward step and that is difficult to handle. It was no different for Alex.

"I went through the same thing when I left in the winter of 1974. The difference in my case was it was my choice to go, but in hindsight I knew I had made a mistake. I got on fine with Jock Wallace, the manager, but didn't get on with his style of football. So I left. Two years earlier I'd been Scotland's Player of the Year, but I was so keen to get away that I jumped at pretty much the first opportunity.

"What I grew to realise is that if I had persevered I would have come through it and would most probably have outlasted Jock at the club – and who knows what would have happened beyond that."

What would Fergie do? That's the question worth asking when faced with one of football's great choices, since he more than anyone appears to have shown a knack of making the right call at the right time.

While he embarked on his managerial mission in 1974, it was a further two years until my father followed the lead and accepted a similar type of challenge with struggling Berwick Rangers. He did so in favour of the option of signing as a player for his old team-mate Ferguson at St Mirren, but there were no hard feelings – Ferguson understood the logic more than most.

Berwick were rock bottom of the Scottish league structure at that point, in the late summer of 1976, and the only way was up. The first season saw Berwick climb to mid-table respectability, the second season they were up to fourth and in the third, 1978/79, the Second Division championship was clinched. While Ferguson was setting about his task at Aberdeen, my father's stock was also rising.

He notes: "What Alex has always done well is to look out for himself – he won't let anyone stand in his way. At East Stirling, he had the choice to stay and finish the job he had started or leave after a few months to step up with St Mirren. He chose St Mirren and carried on climbing the ladder.

"At Manchester United, he didn't stay in the job simply because he was successful. There were times he had to stand up for himself and fight to stay in that position – he did that, and he won. He has always had that instinct.

"In my own case, I started at a similar level with Berwick Rangers – right at the bottom of the Scottish Football League. I stayed for a longer period and had success, winning the Second Division championship and taking the club into the First Division, but chose to show loyalty when I had the opportunity to move on. Bobby Parker, who was chairman at Hearts, was keen to take me to Tynecastle but I loved it at Berwick and couldn't bring myself to leave.

"Looking at it with my head rather than my heart, what I should have realised was that I'd taken Berwick as far as they could go by winning promotion to the First Division –

whereas Hearts were a Premier Division team stuck in the First Division at that time, so there was scope for progression.

"When Alex had the choice between staying at East Stirling and going to St Mirren he grabbed it, because he made a calculated decision about what was best for him and which club offered the chance of improvement.

"The other side of the coin was at Aberdeen, where he had plenty of chances to leave before he did but chose to stay. Had he taken the jobs on offer, at the likes of Rangers and Arsenal, big clubs but ones that were struggling at the time, he could quite easily have damaged his own reputation and found himself on a downward spiral.

"Instead he had the sense to wait for the right one to come up and Manchester United proved to be the perfect fit – it was a club with potential for progress, just as East Stirling had been, as St Mirren had been and as Aberdeen had been. He had the patience and the nerve to wait for that opportunity to come up because that was the one that worked best for him."

Berwick had indeed gone as far as they could. My dad's departure from the job he loved during the 1980/81 season, a campaign that would end with the club's relegation, was the catalyst for a return to the family's roots in the north-east and, despite spells in the Highland League in charge of Peterhead and Huntly, marked the end of this particular branch of the Smith clan's involvement in the senior game.

Regrets? Not really. As my dad notes: "Berwick was a great place to live, the family loved it there, but unfortunately all good things come to an end, particularly in management. There were things going on at the club that I didn't agree with and I resigned. I don't regret that and I've still got a lot of time for most of the people who were involved at that time, I'm still in touch with some of the players. The crowds shot up at that time, there was a real feel-good factor, and hopefully I'm remembered well down there."

The move from Berwick back to the Aberdeen area coincided with the Ferguson-inspired glory years for the city's team. Will Dons fans ever see the likes again? Probably not.

As my father points out, the game has changed beyond all recognition. He said: "I don't think Alex would claim to have some magic formula. You could take him back to Aberdeen now, or any other Scottish club outside of the Old Firm, and he would struggle to repeat the success he had first time around because the financial gulf now is so huge. It is a very different environment now.

"Would he get closer than other managers have managed? Probably, yes, because he has the ability to build teams and to get players to work for him – an ability that every other manager would love to have. I've always been a believer that management is made out to be far more complicated than it actually is. It is down to picking players and making them want to play for you – Alex Ferguson has done both of those things exceptionally well over the years, and that has been the key to his success.

"He finds talented individuals and plays them in a way that allows them to enjoy their football and express themselves. The mistake others have made is trying to hammer round pegs into square holes because they want to play this system or that system – all that does is create unhappy players. Unhappy players rarely make for a winning team.

"Succeeding someone of his stature is an almost impossible job – but that won't stop people from queuing up to do it. Just like Alex had total confidence in his ability, there will be somebody out there who thinks they can do better. Whoever takes over will never equal his record or match his longevity. It just doesn't seem possible."

Chapter 9

IT WAS 1974 and the year that brought the world Magna Doodle and *Blazing Saddles*. It also brought the world a young manager by the name of Ferguson, whose appointment to his first post recorded little more than a blip on the news scale in what was a rather momentous period in world history. In Britain, economic uncertainty gripped the nation causing political unrest and fright among consumers faced with spiralling fuel prices. Almost four decades on, it would appear history is repeating itself and the more things change the more they stay the same.

Despite the apparent political similarities, the world has moved on in those years and progress has brought football kicking and screaming along with it – some would argue for the better, others would say developments have been to the detriment of the game in many ways.

Take little old East Stirling and their quaint home, Firs Park. What was once a neat little ground in the centre of Falkirk, a hive of football activity, is no longer. Progress saw the site flattened in 2012, having been sold to a developer following the Shire's decision to move out of their spiritual home in 2008 to make the short hop to ground-share with Stenhousemuir at Ochilview. In Ferguson's day it was hemmed in by housing, a small club right at the heart of the community it served. By the time the turnstiles clicked for the last time, a retail park had sprung up next door and there was interest from the retail and housing sectors for the valuable piece of town centre land. While the promise of a new permanent home remains, a part of the soul of East Stirling was crushed at the same time as the bulldozers moved in to raze the old stadium to the ground.

Part of Shire's appeal was its gritty feel, well-worn and well-loved. A switch to a shiny new purpose-built ground is never likely to recreate the spirit of old, when the punters watched Fergie's Furies bid to claw themselves away from the lower reaches of the league with a fierce will to win. That was Firs Park at its best.

How about Old Trafford? Well 1974 was of course the year of relegation, Denis Law and that back-heeled goal. It was also the year in which Trafford became an official borough and the year in which perimeter fences were erected at the Theatre of Dreams – the first ground in the UK to have the barriers installed, in a bid to keep exuberant fans at bay. Progress eventually saw common sense prevail and those fences, and the associated danger to supporters that went with them, were removed in time. Long before all-seated stadiums became a necessity, Old Trafford like every other major stadium featured large swathes of terracing that swayed in tune with the massed ranks of the home support on a Saturday afternoon. Now it's one of the world's finest, most comfortable and safest grounds and leaves fans wanting for nothing during their match-day experience.

Since the pain of the drop out of the top flight in that year, Manchester United has been rebuilt on and off the park into the global phenomenon we see today. According to the

Deloitte Football Money League of 2012, United's revenues top £330m per year and the club sits behind only Real Madrid and Barcelona in financial terms. In the 1970s the scale of the business today would have appeared laughable, pie in the sky.

In contrast, the more things have changed at the top of the tree the more things have stayed the same for those scrambling around in the game's undergrowth. When Sir Alex checked in at East Stirling he was rewarded with the princely sum of £40 per week as part-time manager of the perennial strugglers. It was not the money that had attracted him, which is just as well since the bounty was minimal. Earnings from his day, and night, job as a bar owner supported the family.

He could tempt players to the Shire with a slim pay packet containing roughly £20. Today, those pulling on the same black and white hooped shirt that Ferguson's men sported almost 40 years ago have to content themselves with a basic weekly haul of £30. That's progress for you. For the clubs in the lower reaches, if anything conditions have deteriorated and the fact that so many have survived, East Stirling included, is testament to the endeavours of the hardy souls who volunteer their time and energy to the cause. Because of them, young managers and young players have a platform from which to launch themselves into the mad, mad world of senior football. The game is a richer place for it and perhaps the next Sir Alex Ferguson is waiting in the wings for his chance to shine.

Untold riches are the potential rewards – that and a Chevrolet club car. The American manufacturer became Manchester United's official vehicle supplier in the summer of 2012, replacing the previous deal with Audi that had seen Sir Alex behind the wheel of some of the German marque's finest pieces of engineering. In June 1974, just as Sir Alex was embarking on his managerial adventure, a classic piece of Bavarian automotive design was being paraded for the world's motoring press – with the launch of the Volkswagen Golf, the model VW hoped would take over from the Beetle as the popular car of the masses. Surely it would never catch on?

Closer to home, the futuristic-looking Triumph TR7 was unveiled in the same year. It really didn't catch on. Filling up your car was not an expensive exercise, with a gallon of petrol costing the princely sum of 42p as car ownership soared, not least through chart-topping sales of the Ford Cortina – the undisputed nation's favourite.

It was a time for innovation in all sectors of society, including entertainment. Long before anyone was made a TV millionaire, Chris Tarrant bounced on to television screens in 1974 with *TISWAS* – or *Today Is Saturday Watch And Smile*, for the uninitiated. While the show prided itself on its gunk, another mysterious substance was making its debut in this year – the delicious and light Angel Delight. If you didn't fancy the elbow grease required for the perfect modern dessert, the option was to nip out for some fast food with McDonald's opening its first UK outlet in this year, choosing London as the perfect spot.

The capital was also at the centre of a technological revolution as the base for Ceefax, which the BBC transmitted for the first time in this year. In another innovation of the time, Gillette launched the first disposable razor onto the UK market. Times they were a-changing.

As mentioned, *Blazing Saddles* was blowing through the world of cinema – but it wasn't the only option for movie and

SHOOTING STAR: In his Rangers days as a big money centre forward.

LONG WALK: Heading for an early bath after being sent off during a typically fiery performance for Falkirk.

HOT WATER: Sir Alex and his St Mirren assistant manager Davie Provan find time to talk tactics. Provan was not offered the chance to move to Aberdeen.

ON THE UP: Sir Alex during his formative years as a manager with Aberdeen in the 1970s and 80s.

CONQUERING EUROPE: Parading the European Cup Winners' Cup with Aberdeen assistant Archie Knox in 1983.

DOMINANT DONS: The manager with the Scottish Cup after a 4-1 victory over Rangers in the 1982 final.

DARK DAY: Sir Alex as Scotland assistant on the night of manager Jock Stein's death in Wales in 1985.

DECISION MAKER:
Manchester United chairman
Martin Edwards with the young
manager he gave his backing to.

KEY MOMENT: The FA Cup is raised after
victory over Crystal Palace in 1990.

YOUNG PRETENDER: Inspirational captain Bryan Robson's managerial career
has failed to hit the heights.

PRIZE GUY: Silverware has become part and parcel of life for Sir Alex at Old Trafford.

EYE ON THE PRIZE: Brian Kidd and Sir Alex with the Premier League trophy in 1993.

GLORY DAYS: The 1999 Champions League triumph will always be one of Manchester United's crowning glories.

COUNTING DOWN: Sir Alex, pictured during the 1993/94 season, is working towards his 30th year in charge at Old Trafford.

SIDE BY SIDE: Brian Kidd, pictured in 1998, is one of the men to have broken away and tried his luck as a manager in his own right.

THE APPRENTICE: Steve McClaren holds the Champions League trophy aloft with his mentor.

TOP TIP: Carlos Queiroz was the man who had been earmarked as a potential successor to the United chief.

MODERN RIVALS: Sir Alex embraces Roberto Mancini as the two men set about keeping Manchester at the top of English football's ladder.

FRIENDLY ADVICE: Roy Hodgson had Sir Alex's blessing to appoint Gary Neville to his England coaching staff.

TV buffs. *The Return of the Pink Panther* was also launched, along with *It Ain't Half Hot Mum* and prison comedy *Porridge* also materialising. Children's favourite *Bagpuss* was also launched, with an initial run of just 13 episodes, while *The Wombles* used small-screen exposure to catapult themselves to pop stardom with *Top of the Pops* appearances to boot. At the other end of the music spectrum, the Knebworth rock festival was launched – with an inaugural line-up featuring Van Morrison and the Doobie Brothers among others.

The year of 1974 also saw the emergence of a new hobby – streaking. The craze swept the nation and sport was not spared, with cricket and football targeted. Even the Academy Awards suffered at the hands of a streaker.

In politics, it was something of a momentous year for Britain. Conservative Prime Minister Edward Heath took a calculated decision to call a snap election in February, on the back of turmoil in the country. It turned out Heath had got his sums wrong – with Labour winning 301 seats to the 297 scored by the Tory party. After failing to win Liberal support for a coalition, Heath was forced to concede defeat and Labour's Harold Wilson was handed the keys to Number Ten once again.

The election was held against a backdrop of industrial unrest. Economic uncertainty had led to attempts to control the labour market with government-led pay freezes. Rolls Royce and shipbuilding enterprises were also nationalised during a tumultuous period. The average house price in Britain in 1974 was a touch under £11,000 – but prospective home owners did not have it all their own way as the fight for fair pay deals began in key industries, not least mining.

Demand for coal was in danger of outstripping supply and the miners demanded pay to reflect the value of the precious commodity they worked to produce. With a 13 per cent pay rise rejected, an overtime ban followed and a three-day working week resulted in a state of emergency being declared. Heath faced a crisis, and that intensified when the pit workers opted to take strike action. It was the straw that broke the camel's back and the PM called the election, expecting the public to side with him and his party and give a mandate to go to war with the miners. His expectations failed to match reality.

Liberal leader Jeremy Thorpe actually threatened to embarrass both Heath and Wilson, with popularity soaring as the others squabbled. But in the end, the traditional giants won the day and fought for the right to lead the country.

In America, 1974 was no less eventful. Richard Nixon announced his decision to step down from the President's office and became the first man ever to quit the top job. The Watergate scandal had prompted the decision, with tape recordings suggesting Nixon had attempted to influence the police investigation into the issue. Vice-president Gerald Ford was the successor.

All of that was just a sideshow for the 30-something rookie manager setting out on what would, unbeknown to him, prove to be a journey of incredible length and a route scattered with silverware. Football was the main event and he immersed himself in the game.

While he was being selected to lead humble East Stirling, in Germany the world's finest players were assembling for the World Cup finals. Scotland were among that number and the nation benefited from one of the finest squads in its history in the international game.

Led by the understated Willie Ormond, the high profile individuals did not disappoint – beating Zaire 2-0 in the opener before earning a very credible 0-0 draw against Brazil and respectable 1-1 result against Yugoslavia. Though unbeaten, the four-point haul was still not enough to mean progress from the group stage but did ensure the Tartan Army left the continent with their heads held high.

A glance at the team-sheet for the Brazil encounter gives a snapshot of the rude health Scottish football was in as Ferguson took his first tentative steps into management, albeit at an altogether earthier level.

While Ferguson scrambled around in the bargain basement trying to piece together a Shire team, Scotland manager Willie Ormond could shop at the equivalent of Harrods. He had Old Firm legends Sandy Jardine and Danny McGrain patrolling the full-back beats with great aplomb, Manchester United skipper Martin Buchan at the heart of his defence, Leeds United superstar Billy Bremner anchoring the midfield, King Kenny Dalglish providing a goal threat and a young Joe Jordan, who was on target against Zaire and Yugoslavia, adding some bite to the attack.

It was an all-star cast at a time when the production line north of the border was in full flow. Indeed, the Scottish Football Writers' Association took the unprecedented step of awarding the Player of the Year title to the World Cup squad as a whole in the summer of 1974.

The competition had been won by the hosts, West Germany, with a Gerd Muller-inspired 2-1 win over Holland in the final, but there was a sense of satisfaction in Scotland about the country's performance. The fact the Auld Enemy hadn't even qualified, leading to the departure of Alf Ramsey in 1974, made it even sweeter.

They were exciting times to be involved in the game, even at domestic level. The 1974/75 season that Ferguson was preparing for was the last before league reconstruction, with the old First Division contested for the last time as the Premier Division plans were put in place.

Celtic had won the championship the previous campaign, their ninth in a row, but Jock Wallace and Rangers were about to wrest the trophy from their vice-like grip and win the title to bring the curtain down on the traditional top flight competition.

While Wallace could plot for an assault on the inaugural Premier competition, a former Rangers man was laying his own plans in the lower reaches of the game. For Alex Ferguson the attention to detail, ambition and burning desire was no less than for his counterparts at the very highest level. It was 1974, the starting point for his adventure in management.

Chapter 10

HINDSIGHT IN football is a wonderful thing. Those who worked with Alex Ferguson during his first managerial assignment look back with misty eyes at those brief but character-building months in the 1970s and insist they knew from the very first day that they had been touched by greatness in the making.

It was written, they say, in the stars that the inexperienced ex-player who walked through the door of a ramshackle lower league ground in central Scotland and addressed a hot-potch squad of journeymen would one day be mixing with the millionaires of the world game. Easy to say now, but difficult to imagine any of them could really have predicted quite how far their gaffer would travel on the path to superstardom.

It begs the question of whether a new manager really can be judged instantly. All too often we hear coaching unions call for their members to be given more time, berating football club chairmen and boards for being too hasty in their decision-making. Yet if you follow the Sir Alex story to its conclusion, it appears that from virtually the first training session and first match it is clear that a winner had been unearthed.

It is nigh-on impossible to find a dissenting voice when it comes to talk of Ferguson's first dalliance with the art of football management, following his appointment by East

Stirlingshire in the hazy summer days of 1974. The irony is that East Stirling, more than any of the clubs he has touched, is the one that would have justifiable reason to complain. After all, he walked out after just months in charge and in that time did not deliver the type of tangible success that all supporters thrive on: trophies.

Yet the fans and officials at Firs Park, the rather humble theatre of modest dreams the club called home in those days, were able to see beyond those moot points and appreciate what their rookie manager had brought to the table: respectability, organisation, determination...and hope. Ferguson, albeit for a short period, had demonstrated that even the minnows could be competitive with the right man in charge. Unfortunately for the Shire, finding the right man in the decades which have followed has proved to be a struggle and the spirit of optimism fostered by Ferguson has been somewhat eroded by, in the main, barren years since then.

Indeed, in the absence of success on the park the club's greatest claim to fame has become its association with the greatest managerial fairytale football has ever seen. He did it the hard way, a true rags to riches tale that covered the whole spectrum of the beautiful game – including the ugly bits in the less than glamorous surroundings that set the ball rolling at the very outset. Had it not been for those earthy beginnings, had he eased himself in with a comfortable job at one of the big names, then the Ferguson story would not have been complete. Instead he has seen it all, from the bottom to the top.

Like every wannabe manager, getting a toe-hold was the most crucial stage. While the Shire have revelled in their role in the Ferguson story, it could all have been very different – the appointment was not a unanimous one.

It was driven by Willie Muirhead, the chairman at the time and a man who became something of a father figure to Ferguson in time. The other two board members on the selection panel were Alec Forsyth and Ian Crawford, and Forsyth was outvoted in his attempt to body swerve the eventual winner in the race for the job.

Forsyth, the only surviving member of that trio of East Stirling officials, told the *Daily Record* in 2006: "My choice was Davie McParland, who won the League Cup for Partick Thistle against Celtic among other things. But Willie Muirhead and Ian Crawford, who went with me to the Garfield Hotel on the outskirts of Glasgow to make up the interview panel, shouted me down and gave Alex the job on the recommendation of Ally MacLeod, who was then his manager at Ayr.

"He only stayed with us for three months and then Fergie's ferocious ambition to get on took him to manage St Mirren. The Shire got no compensation because we didn't have him on a contract. The reason for that was we couldn't afford to put him on a written agreement in case we had to sack him one day and couldn't give him a pay-off.

"I won't be a hypocrite and tell lies. I didn't like the way he forced the club to put an improved bonus scheme in place for the first-team squad. And I didn't want him paying players out of his own pocket at the same time. That's what he did to get an Airdrie reserve player called Billy Hulston, who was thinking about signing for Stenhousemuir.

"Alex was only with us for three months and yet we finished that financial year with a loss of £17,500. But Fergie always got his way and none of the players ever slouched when he was in charge.

"He used to get them so wound up there was one player sent off within the first 60 seconds of a match for a challenge that could only have been the result of getting over-excited by the manager's pre-match team talk."

Davie McParland would have been the safe choice, with the young upstart representing a significant risk. Given his background as an active trade unionist, there was also every reason to expect the rookie would not be an animal easily tamed. Those factors did not put Muirhead or Crawford off though, no doubt swayed by their chosen man's reputation as a hard worker who was desperate to learn and prove himself.

The recommendations came from the very top, as Forsyth pointed out. Muirhead has since passed away, but as Ferguson made his mark with Manchester United in the 1990s he occasionally was called upon to look back on the good old days by members of the press eager to piece together the jigsaw of the managerial messiah's background.

Muirhead, in a 1999 interview with the *Daily Record*, revealed he only agreed to take the call tipping him off about the rising talent's availability when he was sure the charges were not going to be reversed – the call was coming from Munich after all, and Shire weren't made of money. Far from it, in fact.

He quipped: "I wouldnae have accepted the call if I'd to pay for it, no way son! It was during the World Cup in Germany that the Alex thing came about. We had directors over there and one called from Munich to ask how our search for a manager was progressing. I told him we had done a couple of interviews but no-one was signed up.

"He said he'd met Ally MacLeod in Germany and he had a reserve player who was desperate to get into management. His name was Alex Ferguson. I gave him a call and interviewed him. I knew right away he was different from the other candidates. There was something about him. I offered him the job over dinner with his wife Cathy at a Falkirk hotel. I was pleased to see he was a sensible, family man."

The relationship between the two men blossomed and never faded. Muirhead would often get letters dropping through the letterbox of his home in Falkirk, marked with the Manchester United crest and addressed: "Dear Faither". Muirhead added: "Actually, it was probably me that started all that. I phoned him one day and his secretary asked who was calling. I said, 'it's his faither from Firs Park'. Alex has called me 'faither' ever since."

Ferguson has since reflected about his logic in accepting what looked, on paper, to be an utterly thankless task. But, by his own admission, he did not have clubs banging down his door to give him a chance in the most competitive of job markets.

In *Managing My Life*, Ferguson wrote of his initial impressions of life at East Stirling: "We had a total of eight players on the books and they did not include a goalkeeper, and remind myself that East Stirlingshire had finished bottom of the Scottish Second Division in the previous season, which made them the worst senior team in the country, I had to wonder why I had chosen to launch my management career at Firs Park.

"One simple reason was that my interview with Queen's Park had been a disaster. Ally MacLeod had given me a glowing recommendation. But everybody on the board at Hampden had played with me and in front of the interviewing committee I surrendered to nerves and failed to offer a shred of justification for employing me.

"It was mainly a desire to be courteous that made me accept East Stirlingshire's invitation to talk to them but when I met their chairman, Willie Muirhead, the honesty in his face and the ease I felt in his company persuaded me to take a chance."

East Stirling, still rooted in the lowest tier of Scottish football and perennial strugglers, look back fondly to the brief interlude with Sir Alex. He is credited by club historians with "galvanising" the club and bringing "new-found belief" to his band of merry men. The fact his tenure also included the first victory over town rivals Falkirk in 70 years helped.

It was by no means an easy job. The ability to wheel and deal that he was having to develop in his full-time job as a publican would come to the fore in football too.

Money, or more specifically a severe lack of it, was quite frequently the root of tension at Firs Park.

Ferguson, speaking at a League Managers' Association celebratory dinner to mark his achievements in the game, said: "I'd been in the same position as every manager that finishes playing one day and becomes a manager the next. When I took over the job I had eight players. The chairman, Willie Muirhead, who was a great old man, was a chain smoker and when he had a problem the smoking went quicker. I said: 'Mr Chairman, can I have a list of the players?' and he started coughing, the fag was going at a hundred miles an hour, and the list had eight players and no goalkeeper.

"He said they would have a board meeting and raise some money for me. He came back and said he had £2,000, and I started trawling the free list. My first signing was George Adams. I paid £100 and to this day I think it was too much! But it was great because it taught you how to survive."

How to spend that modest transfer kitty was one of the first big decisions of his managerial career. Ten £200 players? Not a chance – he went for quality over quantity and has never broken that habit since.

Muirhead recalled: "I gave him £2,000 to buy players and went on holiday. He called my hotel after a few days to say he'd bought a player called Billy Hulston. 'How much for?' I asked. '£2,000' said Alex. Go away son. You've ruined ma holiday! I'll call you when I get back."

Hulston, a 28-year-old forward who had played at a higher level with Clyde and then Airdrie, was being courted by other teams – not least Shire's near neighbours Stenhousemuir, then managed by another future Aberdeen boss in the shape of Alex Smith. After talks with Shire's new manager, Hulston had his heart set on joining the Ferguson revolution but asked for time to call Smith and explain his decision. Ferguson denied him that opportunity, telling him he had to sign then and there – sweetened by the offer of £50 from his own pocket to seal the deal. The notes were produced, placed on the table and the all-important signature duly followed. As Hulston has since reflected: "He was such a strong character, so positive. He decided what he wanted and got it."

Experienced players like Hulston were just part of the master-plan. Alongside them the new man wanted young and energetic players who had the engine to play at the tempo he wanted to for the whole 90 minutes – with the added bonus of costing pennies to employ.

Not all of the board saw it that way, with one episode seeing the boss hauled over the coals for spending £40 on a minibus to ferry the youngsters through from Glasgow. Muirhead said: "Eventually, Alex pulled £40 out his own pocket and threw it on the table – then stormed out. I phoned him at home and we met for lunch next day. I begged him to stay and he did.

Later I heard he was ready to chuck football forever that night. I'm glad I talked him round. He could have been lost to football forever."

Some players might secretly have been delighted if the firebrand had walked away. He set high standards for his squad, regardless of the previously low expectations, and would not rest until he had brought an improvement. It meant a lot of hard graft for his new charges, who had their first chance to impress when Tranmere Rovers – complete with centre-forward Steve Coppell – travelled north for a pre-season friendly.

Hulston said: "At Shire, everything focused towards his goals. Time didn't matter to him, he never wore a watch. If he wanted something done, he'd stay as late as it took, or come in early.

"Training was always sharp and enjoyable. He was always right in the middle of things, unlike many bosses back then, who just sat in their office."

He expected total commitment, right down to denying players permission to attend weddings on match-days regardless of how near and dear the subjects were.

Training would go on long into the night, not least if Ferguson's five-a-side team happened to be losing and players quickly noted that their manager chose not to wear a watch. It was only time to leave when the work had been done and done to his total satisfaction.

McCulley added: "He always joined in and would have us playing in the dark until his team won. He was ferocious, elbowing and kicking. We'd say to each other: 'Just let him score and we can all go home,' but it didn't work because if we weren't trying, he knew. He owned a pub in Glasgow called Shaw's Bar and I used to go in after he'd moved to St Mirren. I'd find Fergie inside playing dominoes with all the old men and slamming pieces down deadly serious trying to win."

The competitive action for the new look Shire side started with a League Cup tie against Forfar in Angus. The message to the assembled squad was simple: "Stand up, be counted, demonstrate your desire."

That message got lost somewhere along the way and the young Ferguson strode up the tunnel to address his troops at half-time as they nursed the pain of a 3-0 deficit. The debut was not going to plan.

Player Bobby McCulley, after his experiences in training, was expecting a fiery blast. He said: "Already he terrified us. I'd never been afraid of anyone before but he was a frightening person from the start."

The ear-bashing never materialised. Instead, the learner-boss told his men that they had played well and didn't deserve to be losing. "And another thing – you can win the game," he added.

McCulley said: "He was right in that we had been unlucky, but we thought he was mad."

That match against Forfar ended 3-3, the first sign of his unique ability to manage a situation as well as he can manage a football team. He did not have pots of money to use as motivation – with the Shire bonus scheme promising £5 for a win, £10 for two in a row and £15 for the third. Instead he chose to lead by example, inspiring confidence while at the same time demanding respect.

McCulley told the *Daily Record*: "But he certainly won the respect of the East Stirling dressing room. When he spoke, you listened. We had a big miner in our side, Gordon Simpson, who was afraid of no man, but he wouldn't have dared interrupt the manager if he'd gone off on one.

"He dropped me for a game at Stranraer, which the Shire went on to win just to prove his point, but my disappointment was still festering when we stopped the bus for a bite to eat on the long journey home. I went into the bar of the hotel we were in and ordered a pint. I hadn't knocked the froth off it when he came in and drew me a glance that would have stopped a clock. I pretended the pint belonged to someone else and told Alex I'd been in to look for the toilet."

The 1974/75 season was not an easy one to be an East Stirling supporter, not that the majority before or since have been either. But this one was particularly painful as fierce local rivals Falkirk, situated just a long thrown-in away at Brockville, were on course for the Second Division championship. Shire, at best, could hope for mid-table respectability in the same division that term under their new leader.

However, there was time for some bragging rights to be won. The first match between the two sides fell on an autumn afternoon and Ferguson had a plan. He whisked his players, thought of as the poor relations in the town compared to the big guns of the Bairns, away to a hotel for dinner on the eve of the encounter. The hotel he chose was the same one as Falkirk used, leading to much bewilderment among the assembled opposition players.

The gatecrashers took the opportunity to listen to pearls of wisdom from their boss, who used it as a chance to outline weaknesses among the Falkirk squad sitting just a few feet away. He was meticulous in his preparation for his first derby matching, producing a list of chinks in the Bairns armour. His team won 2-0, against all odds, and for a change the Shire fans could enjoy their Saturday night out on the town.

He was three months into his job by then, and it turned out to be one of the remaining highlights as he was soon on his way to new pastures. In that time crowds had leapt up to 1,200 – a factor that no director looking in from the outside admiringly could afford to ignore. Regardless of some of the Shire directors' misgivings about an apparent disregard for the playing budget, the manager could argue he had paid his own way.

He jumped ship quickly, but it was, according to his trusted chairman at the time, not an easy decision. While the perception is of a ruthless individual, Muirhead countered that by revealing: "Alex was confused. He called Jock Stein and Jock gave him some great advice. Stein said: 'Go to the highest point at Love Street and look down. Do the same at Firs Park. Ask yourself which ground has the most scope for your ambitions.' He was the greatest thing to happen to our club. He won games and doubled crowds. But he was gone after just five months."

Ferguson appreciated Shire's support. In his own book, he recalled: "Willie Muirhead was typically marvellous when I told him I was moving on after just three and a half successful months with his club. In their last match for me, the players produced their best performance since my arrival, a 4-0 thrashing of Alloa, which made delivering my subsequent announcement all the tougher.

"Mute shock was the general reaction until our wing-half Tom Donnelly said: 'You bastard!' Tom was a good lad and showed his disappointment as honestly as he lived his life. I shook hands with all the players and made my way to the boardroom, where I thanked the directors for the opportunity and support they had given me. As I left East Stirlingshire for St Mirren, there was no trace of exhilaration but rather a dull sense of failure, of a task unfinished. I had no right to assume that the players awaiting me at Love Street would serve me as well as the diamonds I was leaving behind at the Shire."

He has never forgotten those days. When Shire were faced with being dubbed Scotland's worst ever team, requiring three points from their final match of the season in 2003/04 to avoid that tag, their one-time boss sent a good luck message, of sorts. It wasn't so much about luck, according to the football doyen. The message read: "Just win".

Shire chief Les Thomson said at the time: "I have kept in regular contact with him over the years and he always has a few words of advice and encouragement when he feels it is needed.

"He always looks for our result on a Saturday afternoon and has certainly not been enjoying our poor run this season. With Manchester United gearing up for the FA Cup Final against Millwall next week, it says a lot for the man that he still has time to think of us.

"It will be a tremendous boost for the lads to know that someone as famous and respected as Sir Alex will be cheering them on."

As it happened, the pep-talk appeared to have the desired effect – Shire beat Elgin City 2-1 and, despite finishing bottom of the Third Division, they managed to beat the record low points tally of Clyde, set way back in 1900, by all of two points.

Beyond motivational snippets, Ferguson has also lent his support to developments in the town where he cut his coaching teeth – first with Falkirk and then as manager at East Stirling.

He returned to cast an eye over Falkirk's new training facilities at Stirling University in recent years, when visiting to receive an honorary doctorate in recognition of his services to sport, and it brought the memories flooding back.

Ferguson told the *Falkirk Herald*: "Facilities are one of the ways to motivate young players and that's something that's been sadly lacking for several years in Scotland.

"When I was a player, and for a while as a manager, they didn't have the facilities. You have to give a young player proper preparation to be a player."

Recalling his Shire days, he added: "We had the pitch. That was it, and we trained on it every day. By the time I left, the club was third in the league, and the players had improved, but the next manager inherited a bad pitch."

By then Ferguson was already in place at St Mirren. Willie Cunningham was the man he had been chosen to replace at Love Street – the man who had given Ferguson a lifeline when, as boss of Falkirk, he recruited him as a player following his departure from Rangers. St Mirren were one place below Shire in the Second Division, but they had potential to do far better than they were at that time. As their SPL status today proves, as well as Scottish Cup success in the years following Ferguson's 1980s tenure demonstrates.

While he spotted the opportunity for progression at St Mirren, Ferguson himself has admitted he failed to apply the same rule of thumb when he subsequently rejected overtures from Aberdeen in 1977 and chose instead to stay with the Buddies.

He said: "Just as East Stirlingshire cannot be a St Mirren, so St Mirren cannot be an Aberdeen and Aberdeen cannot be a Manchester United. Had I recognised that fact when Aberdeen first spoke to me, then I would have saved myself a great deal of heartache."

He eventually got his Dons chance, the following year, but not until he had gone through the obligatory managerial experience of being sacked by St Mirren.

His acrimonious departure from Love Street does not obliterate the good work that had been done, not least in establishing a youth policy that was designed to improve quality and save money into the bargain. A chairman's dream, and a policy that stayed with him at Aberdeen and Manchester United in later years.

Tony Fitzpatrick, one of the youngsters brought through the system, went on to become a Buddies star and would later manage the club. Now proud to see them established back in the top flight, Fitzpatrick said: "St Mirren owe Alex Ferguson an incredible debt. Without a doubt, it was Fergie's charisma that brought and kept players here. Fergie actually set everything off and running. He put St Mirren back on the map again and built a youth policy that was second to none in Scotland at the time."

Ferguson himself told the *Herald*: "There was no money available so we used to bring in young kids from all over the place on Monday, Tuesday and Thursday nights. St Mirren already had a terrific scouting system – led by the incredible 'Baldy' Lindsay – when I arrived, but I increased the network so we had guys working their socks off running round here, there and everywhere prospecting for nuggets. I had more scouts working under me than Baden-Powell."

The network was not fail-safe though. A certain Ally McCoist used to travel through with the manager from their home town of East Kilbride for training at St Mirren, but Ferguson had concerns about his physical size and did not follow up the interest. McCoist, one of the greatest goalscorers ever seen in the Scottish game, enjoys reminding him of that error in judgement.

Just as it had been at East Stirling, money remained an issue at St Mirren. Ferguson explained: "We had so little money I had to approach the supporters' association for their financial help when I wanted to make Dundee United centre-half Jackie Copland my first signing. The transfer fee was £17,000, which was a substantial sum for St Mirren and after listening to me the fans generously put up a loan of £14,000.

"The only way forward, however, was by giving youth a chance. When it came to selling St Mirren to young players or their parents, my assistant and old Rangers team-mate Davie Provan and I promised them two things; that they'd be given the opportunity to express themselves and that no matter their age, if they were good enough then they'd be given the chance of playing in the first team.

"It was also important to me that St Mirren played with a certain style and flair. I was fortunate that so many of them were very receptive to that ideal. Lads like Frank McGarvey, Billy Stark and Peter Weir had great skills and an even greater desire to play the game as it should be played. Then there was Tony Fitzpatrick, who I made club captain when he was still only 18 because of his drive and hunger for information to improve himself.

"Perhaps the greatest satisfaction I derived from my time at Love Street was in providing four players – Fitzpatrick, Stark, McGarvey and Robert Reid – for the Scotland Under-21 team in 1977. That was an incredible achievement for a club outside the Premier Division."

In less than four years with the Paisley Saints, the attendances grew from just short of 2,000 to in excess of 11,000 – partly down to improved performances and promotion, but also down to the manager's determination to stoke community interest. A megaphone became the chosen tool for promoting home games, and it was effective.

The direct marketing, the fall-outs with directors, missed opportunities and difficult choices were all part of the apprenticeship that sent him on his way to another level. Shire and St Mirren had provided the education, Aberdeen would provide the perfect testing ground to put the theory into practice at the very highest level. He was on his way up – the question was who would he take along with him for the journey?

Chapter 11

THE YOUNG man standing in the dole queue was like most others who were alongside him in the line that snaked from the desk in front of him. He had a wife and young family to support, hungry mouths to feed. He had no job, thrown on the scrapheap at the tender age of 31.

Just days earlier all had been rosy in the garden – he had a career with real prospects, an employer with a reputation for looking after its staff, a neat German company car and a boss he respected and got on well with. Then, in an instant, it was all gone. The same boss he admired so much had sharpened the knife and brutally cut him down when he should have been in his prime.

That young man was Willie Garner and the year was 1986. He had been assistant manager to a certain Alex Ferguson at Aberdeen, before being pushed aside in crushing fashion. Now older and wiser, Garner can be found in the plush offices of RBS in Edinburgh, having carved out a successful and challenging career for himself in the financial services industry and wound his way to the headquarters of one of the world's biggest banks in a senior role. Not bad for a humble kid who left school with no formal qualifications, only a burning desire to succeed in football.

Unlike so many who fall victim to football's cruel twists, Garner went on to find a niche for himself in the 'real' world and has little room for regret. Yet, niggling away at the back of his mind, is that most irritating of questions: what if?

What if Ferguson had retained his services, rather than replacing him with Archie Knox in the fateful summer of 1986 – just months before accepting the challenge of swapping Aberdeen for Manchester? What if he had been given the same type of platform at Old Trafford as future international managers Steve McClaren and Carlos Queiroz had? What if Ferguson had shied away from making a decision that he knew would cause untold heartache and stress for an enthusiastic young football coach and his family?

Garner told me: "There's rarely a day that goes by that I don't think about it. I wouldn't say it nags away at me, but it's difficult not to wonder what might have been."

That shouldn't be a surprise. After all, it is difficult to pick up a paper or watch the news on television without some form of reminder of the power and influence that Old Trafford's chief now holds.

He did not get where he is today by being a soft touch. Equally he did not reach the heady heights without help along the way, and on occasion the two factors have merged together in uncomfortable fashion.

Queiroz and McClaren went from the relative sanctuary of a place in the shadows as assistants to Sir Alex Ferguson to the blazing sunlight of life as international managers, propelled from the background to the foreground to take their chances on the biggest stage of all. But for every Queiroz and McClaren there is a Davie Provan or a Willie Garner.

For football fans in Scotland, the names of Provan and Garner will be familiar from their playing days. Provan (no, not his ex-Celtic Sky Sports namesake) was a dependable and committed full-back for Rangers in the 1960s and Garner was a dominant centre-half for both Aberdeen and Celtic in the 1970s and 1980s.

What most will not recall is their part in the Ferguson story. Both men played important roles in sending the great man on his path to managerial greatness, but both were among the many who have fallen by the wayside during that journey. Some by choice, some through the ruthlessness that has been a hallmark of their former employer's career in coaching. Staff have come and gone, but when the time has been deemed right for a change there has been no hesitation in casting able men aside.

While the manner of the departures has been intriguing, the recruitment process has been equally captivating. From his very earliest days in the Scottish game, the choice of assistants have followed a similar pattern. The right-hand men have invariably been low-key individuals, no marquee signings when it comes to the behind the scenes roles. While some have gone on to make a name for themselves, in the mould of Queiroz and McClaren, they have started as relative unknowns to those outside of football's inner sanctum.

Chosen for their football and coaching knowledge? Or chosen because they would not threaten to challenge the boss? Only the man himself knows but his willingness to make changes at the top ensure that there has never been room for complacency for any of those who have fought side by side with him in the trenches.

Looking in from the outside, it is difficult to imagine Ferguson being receptive to his own ideas being challenged. His tunnel vision, the focus that has brought such staggering results, is, after all, one of his greatest attributes. Were he willing to bend or be knocked off course easily then his strength would be diminished, but those who have served in the trenches alongside him insist there is a willingness to take ideas on board.

While a positive contribution to team matters is welcomed, what he has traditionally looked for has been a trusted ally able to share the load on the training field, lead the troops in the day to day work. McClaren was a case in point – a man who had spent his coaching career in the background, but who had a glowing reputation for his ability on the training field rather than as a tried and tested manager in his own right, even if that is the route he has travelled in his post-Old Trafford days.

Ferguson's first ever assistant was Davie Provan, at St Mirren. Provan, a Scotland international, had a reputation as a players' player at Rangers, where he made more than 200 appearances after being recruited in 1958. He was introduced to the first team fold as a teenager and went on to win an array of honours at Ibrox – including being an integral part of the domestic Treble-winning team of the 1963/64 season.

A broken leg in 1967 hampered Provan's hopes of an even lengthier stay with Rangers and he went on to play for Crystal Palace and Plymouth Argyle before winding his way back to St Mirren, where he soon took on coaching duties during Ferguson's successful spell at Love Street. The assistant was later described by Ferguson as being "as conscientious and trustworthy a man as you could ever have at your side".

With those sentiments in mind, when it was time for the manager to move on, Provan must have expected to be following his leader north. Then came the bombshell – the partnership was being dissolved, just at a time when it looked to be taking off.

Ferguson, in his book *Managing My Life*, admitted he let fan power sway his decision after accepting the Aberdeen job. He wrote: "Davie Provan had impressive credentials but I was worried about possible resentment of our shared Rangers connection, something that had been discernible at Love Street, from the boardroom to the terraces. Telling Davie I wasn't taking him with me was difficult but we have remained the firmest of friends.

"My first choice as right-hand man was Walter Smith, who was doing splendid work under Jim McLean at Dundee United, but efforts to negotiate with Jim met a brick wall. So I went for Pat Stanton, who had just ended his playing career. Pat did not have the coaching experience but he had everything else and it was a major extra asset that he had been such an exceptional player for Hibernian.

"I could not have asked for a better lieutenant. It was invaluable to be able to bounce ideas off him as we discussed the merits of the players on our staff and the structure and playing style."

Stanton did not stay for the long term, returning to live and work near his family in Edinburgh, while Archie Knox, his second assistant manager at Pittodrie, was lured south to become manager of Dundee.

That created a vacancy in 1983 for a new coach to join the inner circle – and it was a surprised Willie Garner who got the call.

Garner had played more than 150 games for Aberdeen, although he was away from the club by the time he was singled out for the assistant manager's role under Ferguson. He had played under him previously though, having made his debut for the Dons two years prior to Ferguson's arrival and keeping his place in the side during the key early years of his tenure as boss.

He had been a key man in the 1976/77 League Cup-winning team at Pittodrie an added to his medal collection and after Ferguson's arrival in 1978 when he helped his side to the Premier Division title in 1979/80, switching to Celtic in 1981 in a £46,000 deal. It was just a year later, after losing his place in the Hoops side, that his career began to take an interesting change in direction.

The former Dons star told me: "When I dropped out of the Celtic team, I went out on loan to Alloa to get some games under my belt and right at the end of that month's loan the manager, Alex Totten, left to go to Falkirk. That opened up an opportunity for me, even though I was just 27 at the time. I phoned Alex Ferguson for advice and the message was simple: 'Go for it.' I listened to that advice and took the Alloa job on.

"I think my willingness to do that at such a young age showed that I had a determination to go in that direction, and it obviously stuck in Alex's mind. When I played under him at Aberdeen, I'd always had a willingness to come back in the afternoon for extra sessions and to work with the young boys at the club and he'd obviously taken note of that too. When he was looking for a new assistant after Archie Knox left to go to Dundee, he approached me about taking on the role. I didn't hesitate."

Garner, like his mentor, had enjoyed relative success in his first managerial posting as he protected Alloa's First Division status – mission accomplished.

At Aberdeen, after joining in February 1984, he took those coaching rewards to a whole new level. Continuing to turn out for the reserve side while working alongside Ferguson with the first team squad, Garner won the league and Scottish Cup double in their first season together and in 1984/85 won another championship together. A League Cup and Scottish Cup double the following year proved the partnership was working.

He admits: "Going back to Aberdeen as assistant manager was a real challenge and one I enjoyed. Obviously I had been a team-mate of a lot of the players in the dressing room but it wasn't difficult because of the type of professionals we had at the club – people like Willie Miller, Alex McLeish and Gordon Strachan accepted that I had a job to do and helped me get on with it. The only thing I made a point of doing differently was not socialising with them as I had done when I was a team-mate."

Garner believes his approach as a player had played a part in landing him the assistant manager's role in the first place and he embraced the opportunities in front of him at Pittodrie.

He said: "Alex Ferguson has got a work ethic – to serve with him you have to show the same work ethic, I think that is the quality he looks for above all else. He is a driven, driven man and was no different in that respect at the start of his managerial career than he is now.

"I worked with him when he was a young man, so perhaps he was more raw back then. But I think the basic principles of his style have remained the same, in that he has a tremendous ability to get people to play for him. His man-management skills have always been a major part of his success.

"I'd always had a good work ethic, but when you go in and start working with him you have to up it even further. That meant going to watch games every night of the week, just as he did. Whether that was to scout players or just to observe different systems and methods, it was relentless.

"I put an awful lot of miles on a wee Audi club car that they gave me. When you're based up in Aberdeen it isn't just a case of nipping out to watch a game, there's a lot of travelling involved. I enjoyed it though, it was all part of the challenge.

"We did it day in and day out – it was never a requirement of the job as such, but I certainly felt it was expected. He was doing the same after all."

While the assistant manager's job was varied, one of the main aspects was lending an ear and providing a sounding board for a manager who was still finding his way in the game.

Garner added: "He didn't want a yes man. At the time it was just Alex, Teddy Scott and I who were involved on the football side. We would sit in the manager's room every morning and discuss things and he was always open to debate. He was the manager and the final decision was his, but he expected you to challenge things – whether it was to do with decisions on individual players or how we would do things in training, he would always listen. You had to make damn sure you had a good argument if you disagreed with him, mind you.

"At that time he was young, fiery and thought he knew everything. He didn't know everything though, and deep down, behind the mask he wears in public, I think he knows that. Certainly over the years I'm sure he's come to realise that there's always something you can learn.

"I am sure he would also be the first to admit that as a manager you have to have a lot of luck riding with you, and he has had that. You look back to what he achieved at East Stirling and St Mirren at the very beginning of his career and there wasn't tangible success as such, but he was fortunate that Dick Donald, the Aberdeen chairman, saw something in him and gave him his big break at Pittodrie.

"He has continued to have luck on his side at vital times – two goals against Bayern Munich in the Champions League final in 1999 proved that. Every successful manager will have had the rub of the green at crucial times, it can be a very fine line.

"But he also has an incredible hunger to succeed. He was not a top, top player but he got into a zone where he obviously decided he was going to be a top, top manager come what may. Every day he worked tirelessly to make that happen – and it did."

The regret for Garner is that he was not alongside the boss for occasions like that momentous evening in 1999 or to savour the buzz of leading Manchester United to domestic glory.

He said: "I've been working for RBS for a couple of years and there's a company magazine that goes out to all corners of the globe. The editor got wind of my background in football and ran a story on it, drawing parallels between management in sport to management in banking, and since then I've had people come up to me quite often saying 'would you not rather be working with Sir Alex?'. I would have loved for it to have been me alongside him through it all – I'd have been a millionaire a few times over!

"History shows that it was never likely that he would stick with one assistant right the way through, although I do think if Archie Knox hadn't left Manchester United to go to Rangers then that would have been a partnership that lasted. They were a real team together.

"There have been a few people who have worked with Alex over the years and that has probably been a good thing for him. It keeps it fresh and brings in different ideas and ways of working.

"As a manager he has never shied away from making big decisions – in a sense there's a bit of bravado involved, certainly in the past. Now I sense he probably takes more time and puts more consideration into them.

"A case in point was his decision to drop Eric Black from Aberdeen's team for the Scottish Cup Final in 1986. Alex had found out that Eric was talking to Metz about a move to France at the end of the season and said 'unless he changes his mind he's out'.

"I tried to talk him out of it, as did Teddy Scott, and the logic was simple: Eric was a player who scored goals in cup finals, he had a great track record in the big games. But Fergie didn't care – he was stubborn like that, he felt Eric had gone against him and against the club and wasn't going to stand for it. He went through with the threat and dropped him – John Hewitt, his replacement, scored against Hearts minutes into the final, we won the game and that was that. He had been proved right not to worry about dropping Eric.

"I was on the receiving end of one of those big decisions, when he replaced me with Archie Knox when Archie left Dundee in 1986. Alex had been away with Scotland at the World Cup in Mexico and had left me to plan for pre-season. When he came back he called me into a meeting, which I just presumed was to discuss preparations for the season. Instead he told me he was letting me go.

"I had a wife and children to support, all of a sudden I was out of a job and had nothing to fall back on – no contract, nothing. The club car was taken back, within a day I'd lost everything I'd worked for.

"For the first time in my life I had to sign on the dole. I was standing there at the Buroo, waiting in line for my turn with everyone staring at me. The day before I'd been in one of the top jobs in Scottish football, but I had no income now and had no choice.

"As it happened, I was only out of work for a week. That was the first and last time I had been unemployed. I got a job as commercial manager with Cove Rangers in the Highland League and then went on to work in financial services with TSB.

"I had left school with no qualifications, all I'd ever thought about doing was playing football, but because I was still a well-known face in Aberdeen it gave me a foot in the door and I ended up selling pensions, life insurance and learning as I went along. It was the start of a long career in the industry and I worked up to a high level with Lloyds before going on to work with RBS. I really can't complain because I've had two very rewarding careers, first in football and then in finance.

"At the time it was difficult to see the positives – I was devastated. I knew at the time a couple of big, big clubs had been sniffing around him and there was obviously a good chance I would have gone with him if he had moved.

"I didn't agree with the decision to replace me and I didn't particularly like the man because of what he had done to me – but I never lost respect for him. He hadn't been shy about taking on the newspapers at that time and there were a few of the tabloids gunning for him – I was offered good money to do hatchet jobs by a couple of papers, but I never did that for the simple reason I had too much respect for him. I'm glad I didn't go down that road.

"In later life I had to make similar decisions myself, tough ones, both in football and in banking – so I have seen the other side of the coin. I know it couldn't have been easy for him, but he had to do what he thought was best for him and for the club.

"I wouldn't class Alex as a friend, simply because I don't see enough of him to say that, but we'll always speak when we meet and he will always know what I've been up to. He's like that, he never loses track of people or forgets them."

As a footnote, Ferguson wrote in his autobiography: "Completing qualification for the Mexico finals involved going out to Melbourne and securing a result against Australia and that kind of absence on international duty deepened my doubts about my choice of Willie Garner to succeed Archie Knox as my assistant at the club.

"Willie, who had been Aberdeen's centre-half, was a lovely lad and possessed good qualities, particularly his knowledge of the game. But he was young and was, at that stage, far too easy-going to suit my ideas about management, I like the hungry ones who are always on the go. In the eyes of the older players, Willie was still one of them and he found it hard to command the necessary respect.

"If I had acted sooner to replace him with a more authoritative assistant, my international commitments would have done less to undermine Aberdeen's bid for a treble of championships. On my return from the World Cup finals in Mexico, I decided that I could not continue with Willie Garner as my assistant.

"He was too young for the responsibility attached to the job. I am glad that Willie has not harboured any grudge towards me over the action I had to take. Archie Knox was keen to come back and that was, of course, the ideal solution for me."

Garner still puts the battling qualities he displayed on the park to good use. I spoke to him as, in his role as part of the communications team at RBS, he fought fires in the aftermath of the collapse of the bank's computing system in the summer of 2012 which left customers, including those of NatWest, without access to their cash. That began on the same day as ratings organisation Moodys downgraded RBS along with other British institutions – nobody said life post-football would be dull or lacking in challenges.

Chapter 12

I T WOULD be a brave or foolish man who opted to walk away from life as part of Team Ferguson. Football's history books are peppered with examples of those who have made that bold move. Most, it is fair to say, have gone on to have success, albeit often after following a circuitous route. Others have, through a mixture of circumstance and choice, faded away and have watched the Sir Alex roadshow from a distance – no doubt left to wonder what could have been if they had stayed by his side.

The fact a succession of men have made the choice to move away and stand on their own two feet hints that living in the shadow of football's knight is a task that takes a certain personality to manage on a long-term basis. While Ferguson quite understandably has been the figurehead and the recipient of huge plaudits, not to mention his Buckingham Palace date to assume his lofty position in the British Empire, those who have worked side by side have done so quietly, efficiently and without the same adulation or reverie reserved for their gaffer.

So it is not entirely surprising that, in time, most have taken that difficult decision to turn their back on the promise of annual success for the challenge elsewhere and the opportunity to put their own name up in lights.

Could it also be that working with a perfectionist, and one with a temper notoriously short, also has a limited shelf-life? There have been no public fall-outs or frustrations voiced from coaches and few players would criticise the man with the Midas touch. But many would admit that Ferguson is a hard task master and a difficult boss to please, something that spans not just the playing staff but the entire football department and beyond. Detail is king, commitment is a given and compromise is simply not an option.

Compare and contrast to the likes of Arsenal, where Pat Rice worked alongside Arsene Wenger as assistant for 16 years prior to his retirement in 2012, and there's evidence that partnerships can go the distance if the circumstances are right. Wenger, for all his frequent displays of petulance, is without the same fiery temperament as his Scottish rival.

That temperament must make the process of walking away from Ferguson all the more testing. Would you fancy knocking on the office door to inform him that you felt the grass was greener elsewhere? Oh to be a fly on the wall of some of those meetings. Some have parted on good terms, others less so. On occasion there has been a compassionate response to the parting of the ways, sometimes a stony reply and indication of a feeling of betrayal. Sometimes there has been an acceptance that an individual has had to move on to better themselves.

And the one accepted rule in football is once you cross Ferguson once, there's no going back – so making that decision is a make or break moment in any individual's career.

When Pat Stanton called time on his short spell as assistant manager of Aberdeen in 1980, he had no inkling of what lay in store for his gaffer. But football was not at the forefront of his decision to quit, with family reasons the decisive factor for the former Scotland star's switch away from the north-east and back to his native Edinburgh.

Ferguson said of Stanton's departure: "It was a terrible disappointment to me. I loved Pat. He was a truly honest and trustworthy lieutenant. Even now, when I think if him, it is always with immense fondness."

Stanton, who had been a key man for Hibs and then Celtic, remained in coaching. He served as manager in his own right at Cowdenbeath, Dunfermline and his first love, Hibernian, in the years that followed his Pittodrie exit.

Whereas his former sidekick went from strength to strength with the Dons and then Manchester United, Stanton had less joy. The dream job at Easter Road proved to be something of a nightmare – at one stage he resigned and was then reinstated again in the space of 24 hours in what, from the outside, appeared to be a row about interference from the boardroom in decisions on playing matters.

That was just eight months into his time at Hibs, but he lived to fight another day. It was in September 1984 that he eventually called time on his tenure, once and for all, after watching the Edinburgh giants slump to the foot of the top flight. He said at the time: "I don't want to apportion any blame. The players have worked hard but things just haven't worked out."

And that's the thing with the management game, it is wholly unpredictable. He returned to his day job as a publican in Edinburgh, left to ponder whether he would have been better served biding his time with his old friend Sir Alex and seeing where that took him? In hindsight, yes.

He became the first assistant to walk away from Ferguson – his replacement at Pittodrie, Archie Knox, became the second. Knox had been appointed. successor to Stanton in 1980, having been lured from the relative obscurity of the manager's job at lower league Forfar to join the Dons staff. After a playing career that had taken in Dundee United, St Mirren and Forfar he was a different animal to Stanton. He had a lower profile, but a fierce competitive streak to match that of Ferguson.

Knox spent three and a half years at Aberdeen, including the high of the European Cup Winners' Cup success in 1983, before he made the decision to walk away in December 1983, to accept the invitation to take over as manager at Dundee. Still only 36 at that point, Knox said: "I've gained tremendous experience at Pittodrie but I have not been under direct pressure and now is the time for the ulcers."

Making the leap and cutting the strings with one of the most successful clubs of the era, and most powerful managers, could not have been as simple as Knox made it sound. The two had forged a strong bond, built upon a common sense of purpose. That aside, the manager was adamant they were two very different people.

In *Managing My Life*, Ferguson pointed out: "We had our disagreements but in the main we got on well together and my respect for him was huge. It was said that we were too alike but that was nonsense. We had practically nothing in common other than a burning desire to succeed and the energy to work whatever hours our jobs demanded.

"We drove everywhere and anywhere to watch games and, when Aberdeen became the first club in Scotland to start coaching clinics outside its own area, we travelled to Glasgow once a week to tutor promising youngsters at Helenvale, an all-weather pitch that happened to be next door to Celtic Park. Maybe that was something else that Archie and I shared – cheek."

The separation proved only to be temporary, with Knox realising the error of his ways and returning to Aberdeen to reclaim the assistant manager's role from his successor Willie Garner in the summer of 1986. It proved to be impeccable timing on his part, with the jump to Manchester United just months away. When the Old Trafford switch happened, Knox was at Ferguson's side as they embarked on an exciting new chapter.

It looked as though the team was unbreakable, after the previous Dundee dalliance, but what neither man had bargained on was the influence of another hugely respected figure in the Scottish game.

Walter Smith, who had been a team-mate of Knox at Dundee United, had been appointed boss of Rangers in 1991 and he needed a right-hand man. Knox was the one he wanted and the prospect of working at Ibrox was too good for him to turn down. Being rejected once was acceptable to Ferguson. For it to happen a second time touched a nerve with him, and he first twigged that something was afoot after United's European Cup Winners' Cup semi-final win against Legia Warsaw.

He wrote: "I noticed that Archie, usually the life and soul of the party, was rather subdued. I was slightly puzzled, but not worried. We all have quiet moments when private preoccupations make us withdraw from what is happening around us. The next day the cause of Archie's quietness became

crystal clear when I received bad news in a call from Walter
Smith, who had just been appointed manager of Rangers. He
told me that Archie had accepted his offer of the assistant
manager's job at Ibrox.

"I consider Walter a good friend and it was difficult to fall
out with him over the approach he had made. 'I have to do
what will be best for Rangers and will give me the maximum
chance of being successful,' Walter said, and I couldn't argue
with that. When I spoke to Archie it was obvious that the
financial package at Ibrox was well above what we were
paying him but I wasn't prepared to give up, so I spoke to our
chairman about an improved contract.

"Over the next 24 hours I did my utmost to keep Archie and
in my several discussions with him I stressed the attractions
of being part of a European final against Barcelona. 'You may
never be involved in such a match again,' I said. I thought that
argument would persuade him to stay at least until after the
final in Rotterdam, but he was set on going quickly.

"Many people have drawn fanciful conclusions about our
subsequent relationship and some have suggested that Archie
and I haven't spoken to each other since the parting. That is
absolute nonsense. It is true that I was disappointed. We had
come through difficult times at Old Trafford and I felt he
should have stayed with me to see our efforts reach fruition.

"What must also be said is that for some time before he
left we had not been as close socially as we were at Aberdeen,
when we went out together every weekend. Away from work,
we seemed to drift apart as his friendship with Brian Kidd
developed. But I believe our friendship was still strong. The
disappointment, however, did linger with me for a while and

I found it hard to come to terms with his departure. People may imagine that a manager in my position has the skin of a rhinoceros and can shrug off any setback effortlessly, but nobody is unbreakable.

"Archie's decision to go did make me feel vulnerable for a while but there was never any bitterness in my reaction. I have no time for that. My priority was to ensure that his leaving did not affect the strong team spirit within the club."

For those who worked under both men at Aberdeen, there was no doubt the dynamic was one worth trying to protect. Neil Simpson, a hero of the 1983 European team at Pittodrie, was reunited with Knox when the latter was appointed assistant to Craig Brown at the club in 2010. Simpson said at the time: "Archie is the best coach I've ever worked under. He is a great motivator, his training is excellent and is always game-related. But he's also good around the dressing room.

"He was a huge part of the success achieved under Alex Ferguson. In terms of bringing youngsters through, he was outstanding. Three or four afternoons each week, he'd have you back for extra training and demanded standards."

Finding the right man to replace Knox at Old Trafford in 1991 presented a conundrum for Ferguson. In Scotland he had looked close to home, but by the time he was working south of the border the perspective would have to change. Knowledge of the English league and its players would be pivotal.

As it happened, Ferguson turned to a man already on the staff. Brian Kidd, who had been working in a community coaching role and then the youth academy, stepped up to the plate and became a significant influence on first team affairs.

The path did not always run smooth for the pair, with friction along the way.

Ferguson wrote in *Managing My Life*: "The promotion of Brian Kidd in August 1991 into the assistant manager's job vacated by Archie Knox was an instant success, and we soon forged the strong alliance that was to prove so fruitful."

The relationship was dented when murmurs of discontent from Kidd began to surface, but Ferguson stuck by his man. Kidd even gained a new improved contract during the period of uncertainty.

Eventually it was the lure of a manager's job in his own right that broke the bond, with Kidd accepting the post at Blackburn Rovers in 1998.

Ferguson added: "He had proved himself an outstanding coach who was meticulous in his preparation for training. I had always recognised, and made a point of acknowledging, the important role he played in getting the team ready for games. The seven years we spent working together was a golden time for Manchester United. His forte was training players and with us he revealed a gift for getting close to them. Each individual in the squad came to feel that Kiddo wanted him in the team.

"In fact, when I gave Brian his say about who should play, naturally he had his favourites. Not surprisingly, they were mainly lads he had brought to the club when he was youth development officer. Just as his predecessor, Archie Knox, gave me splendid backing while I was laying the foundations in my first five years at Old Trafford, so Brian was an integral part of the success that came in a flood afterwards.

"Along with his achievements as a player, his excellent contribution as my assistant assured him of an honoured place in the history of the club.

"My relationship with Brian was a good one and, though there were periods in the summers of 1995 and 1998 when his tendency to moan to other people around the club left me feeling slightly undermined, I don't believe he behaved that way outside the confines of Old Trafford. I preferred to see it as just a quirk of his nature.

"I hoped Brian would not be disloyal to me after what I did for him. When I plucked him away from community work in Manchester he was earning about £10,000 a year and when he left United his pay bore no resemblance to that figure."

Just as football has a habit of doing, the switch to Ewood brought about an unfortunate set of circumstances. It was left to Manchester United, courtesy of a 0-0 draw against Rovers at Ewood Park, to relegate Kidd's team from the Premiership in his first season.

Ferguson observed: "It was fatal for them and I did not relish going into Brian's office afterwards. Fortunately, he was in tremendous spirits, happily trading banter with my staff and recalling the good times he had among us in the past. I could not help wondering if he regretted separating himself from all that."

The players Kidd left behind at Old Trafford certainly regretted his decision. He had huge support within the star-studded dressing room.

Paul Ince, not always the easiest to please, said: "Kiddo was and still is a fantastic coach. His knowledge of football is second to none and, above all, he is a top, top person.

"At United, he was always the person you would turn to when you had just been slaughtered by the gaffer. Kiddo would be there to put an arm around your shoulder and he would make it feel not quite as bad as it was. That's a great trait to have."

Paul Parker, another to have played under the duo in the 1990s, shared the same opinion. Parker said: "His [Ferguson's] great strength is that he's always had good people next to him. When you look at the fact he had a Brian Kidd next to him, it made such a difference in my time.

"He's a man that needs a bit of help. For all his knowledge and everything, you can't be like a Sir Alex and be such a knowledgeable man in football, in life and everything else and be a tactician as well."

Parker's assessment is perhaps harsh, to cast aspersions about the manager's tactical nous appears curious. But then he was there and we were not.

Kidd had experience of playing for Manchester United and playing at the highest level as a member of the 1968 European Cup-winning team. That gave him kudos, but it was his approach to his various roles within the club that won him friends.

His seven-year spell as assistant manager brought four league championships and two FA Cup wins. Prior to that, he had spent three years heading the youth development programme and took Ryan Giggs, Paul Scholes, Nicky Butt and the Neville brothers under his wing.

Gary Neville wrote in his autobiography: "Appointing Kiddo to head up the academy was a master-stroke. The great thing about Kiddo was his ability to make you feel at ease.

"Right from the start, he was your mate, the guy always looking out for you, his arm round your shoulder. I loved the way he was always happy and buzzing. Kiddo was the good cop compared to Eric Harrison, a scary Yorkshireman who became a huge presence in our lives as schoolboy trainees."

Harrison admired Kidd's bravery in severing his Old Trafford ties to take on the Blackburn job, but believes it represented an error in judgement. He said: "Brian had his feet in the water at Blackburn and whether it could have worked somewhere else, you don't know. But it always seemed to me that coaching was his forte. There's a big difference between coaching and managing. There are not many managers who go out and coach. Their thing is man-management.

"They've got to make sure the team is all pulling in the right direction, making sure there are no cliques and they know what it means to play for Manchester United. I've never fancied it. I know what my strengths are and they are on the training pitch."

Kidd has since returned to doing what he does best, with roles in the England camp as well as at Leeds and Portsmouth before being appointed assistant to Roberto Mancini in 2009 to join the blue uprising in his home city. The results were clear for everyone to see, with Kidd helping to steer Manchester City to the title in 2012 and get one over on his old boss. It took a while, but he proved in the end that there is indeed life after Manchester United and Alex Ferguson.

Archie Knox had been predictable while Brian Kidd had been safe. After those two options had walked out the front door of Old Trafford never to return again, there was little indication as to where Sir Alex would turn next. He had the pick of world football, not to mention a string of Manchester United old boys waiting in the wings for the call to be part of the team.

It transpired the answer did not lie within Old Trafford, nor was it to be found in a far flung location. No, the solution lay a short cross-country drive away in Derby.

Steve McClaren was not a household name, not yet at least. He had not played at the highest level or savoured the rush of international stardom. Steve McClaren had not managed in his own right or sampled football on foreign shores. But Steve McClaren was the man picked out for greatness by a man in need of an assistant.

He had been plucked from Derby County, where he assisted veteran manager Jim Smith, after an exhaustive search by Manchester United. Eric Harrison, who had been a trusted member of Ferguson's backroom team when he served as a youth coach, and Les Kershaw, another key man as youth academy director, were tasked with scouring the land to find the best man for the job.

The criteria set out by the manager was simple: the perfect candidate would have undisputed coaching ability and, crucially, a tireless work ethic.

They set about the job with vigour and looked at all manner of potential recruits, young and old. Time and time again they came back to the same man: Steve McClaren.

Ferguson made his own discreet enquiries and was pleased with the response he received from those he trusted, so he decided to make the move.

Derby proved easy to deal with and an agreement was struck to form a new partnership, with just 36 hours elapsing between the first approach and the ink drying on the contract.

Smith was disappointed to lose his talented young operative, with a glowing reputation for innovation, but knew he could not stand in the way of such a momentous step forward.

Ferguson later remarked: "I was delighted by how swiftly Steve stamped his personality on the job. He has deeply impressed me and I expect him to go on to great things."

Jim Ryan, the reserve team coach, had been filling the void temporarily after Kidd's departure but McClaren was seen as the long-term solution.

He had served as a youth development coach at Oxford United and in the top flight with Smith at Derby. Now he was about to move to a whole new level.

When asked about his move, McLaren admitted: "It's all happened pretty quickly and my head is still in a spin."

It was entirely understandable, but he was delighted with his "great opportunity" and ready to get stuck into the new duties – while learning from the master. Already he was being touted as the new heir apparent for a manager who was expected to spend three or four more years in the hot-seat before retiring.

And then the bombshell came. When the manager made his decision to retire from football in time for the start of the 2002/03 season, it appeared too soon for the young McClaren to be considered a genuine contender. The apprenticeship had not been long enough.

So he took the escape route presented when Middlesbrough offered him a managerial opportunity in 2001, in preparation for the threat of being left out in the cold when Ferguson stepped down at Old Trafford. McClaren left in what was described as a "very difficult decision" ... Ferguson did not eventually retire and McClaren jumped before a push that never materialised.

Writing in the *Observer*, McClaren said: "Having spoken to Sir Alex Ferguson, he was adamant that this would be his final season. Am I surprised by his decision to sign a new three-year contract as manager this week? Not really, no. Knowing the man, I think he looked at things and realised he had the passion, enthusiasm and love, not just for football, but for Manchester United, for the club itself.

"If you are a typical football manager, changing clubs every two or three years, then the travelling around, the settling in again in another place and the rigmarole of building another team from scratch, are all factors that might dissuade you from staying in the profession. None of that is the case here.

"He has been at that club for 15 years and it is in his blood, it's part of him. You can never get a club like United out of your system. I know leaving was the biggest wrench in my football life and I had been there just a couple of seasons. I read Sir Alex quoted recently as saying that once you've been at Manchester United in some capacity, there is nowhere else better to go.

"I know how much he means that. It would have been very, very difficult for Sir Alex to have given all that up, to have got United out of his system, a club where he has done all the groundwork and gained the respect and popularity of everyone.

"But do not think this is one of those instances where he could not bear the thought of long years of retirement. He has a whole host of outside interests: the racehorses, a love of wines, a passionate interest in politics – try talking to him about Scottish history.

"He could have filled his hours very productively and enjoyably. But there are two problems with that. One, he has Manchester United running through his veins and, two, he has passionate views on when this team of his is going to peak. We talked about it often.

"Look at the make-up of the side: the Nevilles, David Beckham, Paul Scholes, Nicky Butt and Ryan Giggs, who have all come through the ranks. There is Ole Gunnar Solskjaer, and now you have Juan Sebastian Veron and Ruud van Nistelrooy. And, of course, although a little older, there is Roy Keane who has just committed himself to United for another four years. If all these players were coming to the end of their careers and there was a major rebuilding job ahead, it would be different.

"What there is is the nucleus of a terrific team. When this team will peak it is hard to say but, with many of the key players entering that 26-30 age bracket, the next three years are going to be very, very big for them.

"The money made available to Sir Alex for van Nistelrooy, Veron and Diego Forlan this season will also have influenced his decision. The one thing the gaffer always talked about in his aim to make ground on the best in Europe was the ability to spend big on world-class players. Now the club have the spending capacity and have shown their willingness to compete with the biggest clubs in Europe when maybe that willingness was not always there before.

"So, if Sir Alex can bring in a van Nistelrooy, a Veron, to strengthen the side, you have what he probably feels he needs to take United to a whole new level. That's one of the things we always talked about, and resources were the only way to do it. Now he has those resources, he has the opportunity and is probably thinking, 'Why give it to somebody else? Why not finish the job myself?'"

McClaren had spent a relatively short time working in Ferguson's company, but he had seen enough to be able to extol the same virtues that so many others had after lengthier periods of service.

He took many lessons from his time at Old Trafford, some basic in concept but vital in practice.

He added: "Sir Alex is the last of a dying breed – of that there is no doubt. By the end of his new contract, he will have been in charge at Old Trafford for the best part of 20 years and we will never see the like of that again, not at this level. Maybe, as in the example of Dario Gradi at Crewe, a coach will be given the time to develop a club but, at United's level, the pressures, the stresses, are far too great.

"People have to concentrate only on the first team to achieve immediate results. There is no time to develop the reserves as Sir Alex has done at United. And if the results don't come, a new manager comes in, he has different policies and any hope of continuity at the club is lost.

"Another of my former clubs, Derby County, who face United today, are a case in point. They have had three managers this season and, while change is obviously sometimes essential, that sort of environment makes continuity and planning impossible. One other thing you can never discount with Sir Alex is his hunger. It is only natural for our enthusiasm to dull as we get older.

"Having worked with him closely, though, take it from me, he is as eager as ever. If there is a prize to be won, he wants to win it. Whether a game of cards, a quiz or a European Cup Final, the man hates to lose.

"A small example. On European trips, it was a tradition to kill the odd hour with quizzes – teams of players versus staff. If we lost, which, I hasten to add, was very rare, it was known for the odd fork to go flying towards the winners. That is the sort of manager United have signed on for another three years and whom I'm looking forward to visiting at Old Trafford again. It's his turn to buy a nice bottle of wine for after the match and I, for one, am delighted that we are going to have a few more years of competing against him."

McClaren, of course, went on to enjoy a successful period in charge of Middlesbrough, including winning the League Cup and reaching the 2006 Uefa Cup Final, before England duty called later that year. Domestic success with unfancied FC Twente in the Dutch league followed and, after his spell in German football with Wolfsburg and back in England with Nottingham Forest, he returned to Twente in 2012. Perhaps the lesson he learned best from his one-time mentor was perseverance.

Chapter 13

H E HAS been described as one of the best coaches in world football, as an innovator, teacher and inspiration. No, not Sir Alex Ferguson but rather Carlos Queiroz – and all of those superlatives were delivered by Ferguson in appreciation of the man he was once proud to call his assistant.

Just as McClaren's rush to the job at Old Trafford had been courtesy of a blindside run, so too had the introduction of Queiroz to the English game. For the first time, the traditionalist Scot had looked beyond British shores to find the right person to sit beside him in the dugout and to join forces on the training field. In fact, it was not only a first for Ferguson but also a first for Manchester United in terms of introducing ideas from an overseas coach.

By that stage the manager had been working in management in Scotland and England for around 30 years. It was time for an injection of fresh thoughts and new methods.

Queiroz had travelled well by that point. Born in Mozambique, it was in Portugal that he had first made his name. He coached the Portuguese Under-20 team to the Fifa World Youth Championship title in 1990 as he nurtured the likes of Luis Figo during the emergence of the so-called "Golden Generation".

His success at that level led to an opportunity with the full national side, although he failed to qualify for Euro 92 or the 1994 World Cup and was left out of work. Not for long.

Sporting Lisbon threw the respected operator a lifeline, but a slip in the run to the title led to his swift departure and led to a world tour as he attempted to rebuild his career.

He coached in America with the New York New Jersey Metrostars and in Japan with Nagoya Grampus Eight before leading the United Arab Emirates and then South Africa. He soaked up the culture of each nation and returned to Europe a more rounded, experienced and knowledgeable operator.

It was that type of well-rounded and lengthy international apprenticeship that persuaded Ferguson to hire a coach who, until that point, had always stood on his own two feet.

He was 49 when he landed at Old Trafford and vowed to bring success to the club. Queiroz said at the time: "It is a great privilege. I am proud and honoured to be given this opportunity. With my full commitment and devotion, I hope to help the club achieve even more success and meet the high expectations of the fans."

Ferguson was brimming with pride as he unveiled his new acquisition, more fulsome in his praise than he would normally be at the time of signing a star player.

The boss said: "I'm really pleased we have Carlos on board. He is someone I've been looking at for quite a while. He has an excellent track record as a manager, particularly with South Africa and Portugal, and is known as an innovative coach. He is also someone who will come in and challenge the players."

Chief executive Peter Kenyon added: "Carlos is a terrific addition to an already strong coaching staff that has helped us collect many trophies over the last few years. In Portugal he was credited with developing the youth system while he has also managed in the USA and Japan."

Backroom boys Mike Phelan and Jim Ryan, together with reserve team coach Brian McClair, all remained in place but there was no doubt that a great deal would be placed on the shoulders of the new recruit.

Ryan Giggs wrote in his autobiography: "The gaffer immediately entrusted him with large amounts of responsibility. He'd train us, prepare us for games, organise the team and decide the things we needed to work on. Some said he had too much influence, but I don't agree. He impressed me from the start."

The import was credited with refining United's formation, leading a modernisation of the once standard 4-4-2 to move with the times. In time he would also become involved in transfer dealings, accompanying chief executive David Gill on the successful missions to recruit the likes of Nani and Anderson. Local knowledge was key.

Initially life was good, Ferguson could rely on his man to do the business. The United boss remarked after Queiroz's arrival: "Carlos is one of the best coaches in world football. His attention to detail, ability to innovate and will to win have been key factors to the team's recent successes. He has played an important role in building and blending the exceptional squad of players at the club."

But it was too good to last. Apparently it was not just Manchester United who appreciated their assistant manager's qualities and when Real Madrid invited him to take charge of their Galacticos in 2003 the outcome was never in doubt.

Queiroz hopped on a fast plane to Spain, pausing only to say: "This is the proudest, happiest day of my life and it's thanks to Alex Ferguson that I'm able to accept this great honour. You can tell him that I love him. I went to speak to Alex personally about this opportunity and it was not a surprise to me that he told me to grab it.

"Alex Ferguson is football itself. No, that's wrong, he is more than football, he has a great sensitivity and humanity that people don't know about. He is a gentleman and a fantastic person. I'm proud to call him my friend."

Like so many who have accepted that particular challenge, Madrid did not prove to be a happy hunting ground. One miserable season, which included an end-of-season collapse, was all he got to prove himself.

At the beginning, the Real experience was a good one – with Queiroz singing the praises of the man he now classes as a friend.

He described Ferguson as a "fantastic human being" and said: "People misunderstand him. In football sometimes we create an atmosphere where people think they can criticise and attack freely, gratuitously. Most of the time coaches are the face of everything that is wrong. Sometimes when coaches put their finger on the right thing people say: 'What is this? He's trying to be a tough guy.'

"I think Alex is a very, very sensitive man and, as a Scotsman, when he needs to say something, when he needs to be strong, he is strong – that's why he is a good manager. In football, you can't just use 'yes' and 'maybe', sometimes in this world, in this football world, you have to say 'no'. Why are people surprised by that? The problem is that everything is so comfortable, so simple, so easy...Maradona, Pelé, Zidane, yes, maybe, nice, easy...No! When it is no we must say 'no', when it is maybe it is 'maybe', when it is yes it is 'yes'."

Read into that what you like, I tend to think it is a tribute to the main man's decisiveness and his strength of character.

Both qualities were not necessarily factored into the equation for Queiroz at Madrid, where he had to adapt to the concept of not having the final say on signings or squad selection. Can you imagine Alex Ferguson operating under those conditions? Queiroz couldn't either.

He said: "Throughout my career working with clubs, signing is something that you as a coach are always there to approve or not. Money talks in this business, but independently of decisions about money – which belong to the club – in a sporting sense, all my life the final word has belonged to the coach...except here (at Madrid).

"When I left Manchester and arrived at Real Madrid I couldn't believe it – the squad was already decided. I didn't have the chance to even have an opinion because I didn't even know a lot of the players. I think, I believe, that next year, learning from what happened this season, Real Madrid should go to normal rules, normal principles in football, where signing players must be approved by the coach's opinion as well."

Madrid didn't change, at least not during the Queiroz regime. Instead they changed the manager and he was out on his ear. When it crumbled around him, Queiroz, like others before and since, found he had a friend to rely upon. Come back Carlos, all is forgiven.

He returned to Manchester United to take up where he had left off, with his role having been filled temporarily by

Ferguson's old friend from north of the border, Walter Smith. He had been out of work following his departure from Everton and provided organisation and experience at a crucial time.

But Queiroz was the one Ferguson was determined to have fighting alongside him in the trenches and he made it happen. He understood the Real Madrid job was too big to turn down, no doubt appreciating his comrade's willingness to take a gamble rather than settle for the easy life as an assistant.

Ferguson had been making moves to appoint Martin Jol, on the back of his accomplishments in Dutch and German football. Jol, who would make his mark in England with Spurs and Fulham, had informal talks with United before the plans were spiked.

Ferguson explained: "I knew Martin and actually spoke to him when Carlos Queiroz left the club. I spoke to him about joining us as assistant manager. While I was talking with him, I had a phone call from Carlos and realised he wasn't happy at Real Madrid so I made moves to bring him back at the end of that season.

"It was unfortunate for Martin but it never stopped his career progressing. He did very well as a coach in Holland and then came to Tottenham. I think he's a terrific manager and his record is good. He's had great experience gathered at Hamburg and Ajax."

The courtship of Jol and appreciation of Queiroz – a man who speaks five languages ably – demonstrates the sea change in Ferguson's approach to the game and his willingness to adapt as the years progress. He recognised the importance of the European influence, not least given the cosmopolitan nature of his own dressing room.

That influence changed the way Manchester United operated, with Ferguson willing to accept guidance during Queiroz's two spells. The second of those ended in 2008, soon after his club side had won the Champions League title.

Speaking after that European triumph, Ferguson said: "What happens after I go is not my domain. But there is no doubt I think Carlos will be here for a long time. As long as me anyway.

"Carlos is improving a lot of things. I am a bit of a dinosaur in that respect. I have recognised progress needed to be made in different areas than I am expert at.

"We have five physios now. I would have been happy with that, plus a nutritionist, a weight coach, a fitness coach. I even brought an orthoptist to assist on the eye training. That kind of thing is fine.

"But the levels we are going to now are unbelievable. Carlos has increased it in all sorts of ways. The entire medical side is fantastic. I don't think there is anywhere better in the world now. That is all down to Carlos' vision of the future which I would not have had."

Right in so many respects, the boss was wrong about one crucial aspect – Queiroz was not there for keeps. That year he switched back to international football when he accepted a second crack at the Portugal job.

That led to the promotion of Mick Phelan to the assistant manager's job, a move that brought the type of continuity that Ferguson had not enjoyed since his partnership with Brian Kidd.

Former United player Phelan had been working as first team coach since 2001 but his promotion to the number two spot also led to a leap for Dutchman Rene Meulensteen, who moved from technical skills development officer to take on Phelan's former role.

Ferguson: "I am delighted that Mick and Rene have agreed to fill these important positions. Mick knows Manchester United inside out, having been associated with the club for the best part of 20 years. He is a very talented and professional coach, whose ability and contribution to the club's success has often been under-stated.

"Rene brings different ideas and experience to the role of first team coach. I believe the two will provide an excellent team to continue the club's willingness to try new ideas and constantly drive for success in an increasingly competitive game."

Phelan, who made more than a century of appearances under Ferguson between 1989 and 1994, had been assistant manager at Norwich City during a coaching apprenticeship which eventually took him back to Old Trafford in 1999.

While life settled down in England, for Queiroz it was not all going to plan. He qualified, if only just, for the World Cup in 2010, before an inept performance left him open to criticism – including from poster-boy Cristiano Ronaldo. It went from bad to worse as he was charged with insulting doping officials, a matter that led to a disciplinary hearing as he battled to save his job.

In a time of need, there was only one person to turn to – step forward Sir Alex, who travelled to provide a character witness for his former colleague.

Giving Ferguson the perfect opportunity for the last word on the qualities of the man he had put so much faith in, he said: "He's a fantastic coach and teacher, and his main purpose in life is to develop young people, to inspire them and to make sure they turn out good human beings, so that's the reason I'm here to support him. I know him well and he's a great man of great dignity. Carlos is one of the good guys."

Queiroz, most recently coach to Iran, may have walked out on Ferguson twice – but he never dented their relationship. As others will testify to, it is an achievement worth noting.

Chapter 14

A S CARLOS QUEIROZ knows, friends in high places can be a vital weapon in any football manager's armoury – and they don't come any higher than the manager's office at Old Trafford. What many have discovered is that the man occupying that seat of power is not the cold and calculated individual that his public persona may suggest.

For friends in need, Sir Alex has turned out to be a friend indeed. Whether through loaning players, providing testimonial opposition or providing a shoulder to cry on, there's a long list of examples of the more charitable side to the character of one of sport's iron men.

People who you might imagine have been lost in the mists of time have received unexpected invitations, with out of sight not necessarily equating to out of mind. Those whose relationships appeared to have ended decades earlier have found themselves, in dark times, being brought back into the fold and helped back on their feet – not always with grand gestures, but sometimes it is the thought that counts. Things that cost not a penny, with the only expense being time, have proved the most valuable to the recipients.

Neale Cooper may not be a household name in Manchester, but the experienced lower league manager has a lot to thank the city's most decorated football club for. Cooper was, as every

Aberdeen supporter knows, a rising star of Alex Ferguson's giant-killing Dons team of the 1980s.

He was just 16 when he was plunged in at the deep end, making his debut in senior football for his home town team, and went on to win the European Cup Winners' Cup as part of the most legendary of all the Pittodrie teams. In the summer of 1986 the bond between the young protege and his father-figure of a manager was broken when the fiery midfielder was sold to Aston Villa.

Unusually, Cooper departed with the full backing of a boss who had always been a major influence on him – with Ferguson believing a fresh start in a different league would free his man from the shackles of conflict with Scotland's referees.

Naturally the pair would cross paths as the years progressed, but they did not work together following their amicable split in the 1980s. Ferguson followed the same path south shortly afterwards while Cooper returned north, first as a player with Rangers and Dunfermline and then as manager with Ross County as the northern minnows made the transition from non-league football in the Highland League to the senior grade after entry to the Third Division.

Cooper, having learned from the best, put his stamp on the club and took them steadily from the Third Division, through the Second Division and on into the First Division. It was there that his team's progress stalled – with the dream of promotion to the SPL not realised until 2012, long after his departure – and frustration crept in. In November 2002 he took the heartbreaking decision to walk away from the project that had enveloped his life, fearing he had reached the end of the road.

It was an emotionally charged period in Cooper's life, with his heart-on-sleeve approach as a player mirrored in his managerial style. Admitting defeat and tendering his resignation was a shattering low for a man who had enjoyed more than his fair share of success in the game, not least during the glory days at Aberdeen. He was tearful, he was questioning what the future held after a lifetime spent in the only profession he had ever known. He needed his friends more than ever.

What Cooper may not have anticipated was that one of the first of those friends to extend a hand and pick him up from the canvas after the blow of his first experience of the brutality of life in management's boxing ring was Sir Alex Ferguson. A call from Old Trafford got Cooper back on his feet and ready to fight another day, with the offer of a stint coaching alongside Sir Alex gratefully accepted. It was purely a voluntary arrangement, no employment offered or sought, but it was a gesture that meant more than any bulging pay packet ever could.

As a journalist covering the Highlands as part of my patch during that time, I experienced at first hand the way Cooper had taken events at County to heart. I also discovered how much the Manchester United 'therapy' had impacted upon him. He could have turned his back on management had it not been for that turn of events – the game is a better and happier place for his decision to build on the success he had enjoyed at County.

In his capacity as a newspaper columnist at the time, with the *Press and Journal*, Cooper wrote: "It is at times like these that you realise who your friends are. The past week has taught me that I am lucky to have the support of so many good people.

"Since I announced my decision to resign from Ross County on Monday, my phone has been red hot with folk phoning to wish me well.

"I have a lot of good friends, not only in football but in my home town of Aberdeen, and now more than ever I appreciate those friendships.

"On that note, only a week ago I had a chat with my old mate Alex McLeish at Rangers and he'd virtually agreed to lend me a couple of players once the transfer window had opened again after the new year. Of course, all that will now go by the board but Big Eck is a great friend and I really appreciated the thought.

"I've also been asked by several different clubs to join them for a week and chill out but football will have to take a back seat as I get my own life together. There is one offer I do intend to take up once I have had a break.

"My phone rang just a minute after signing the paperwork to resign my position as manager. It was Manchester United boss Sir Alex Ferguson calling to say that he'd seen Saturday's result and was phoning to give me a bit of support. I told him that he was about 60 seconds too late.

"Before he rang off, Fergie advised me to take a wee break in the sun to gather my thoughts and then join him at Manchester United for a week or so. That's just what I intend to do – maybe I'll be able to show David Beckham how to take a free kick. Alex has all the experience in the world and he said that he would help me as much as he can.

"Lately, the pressure on me has been intense but only a few days down the line and already I feel that a great weight has been lifted from my shoulders.

"There is no bitterness in me – that's not my style – but in recent times I've been losing some of the characteristically Neale Cooper strengths. I was no longer the happy-go-lucky, laugh-a-minute guy I have been since I was a lad at school. I love a laugh more than anyone and when that went it was a big loss. I now need to get back to being the person I used to be."

He went away and sure enough spent time working alongside his old boss. He fell back in love with football and returned to management, enjoying spells since then with Hartlepool (twice), Gillingham and Peterhead.

Now, more than ten years on, Cooper can reflect with objectivity about the role his old gaffer had to play in helping him back on his feet. He also has his own views on the motivation behind it, believing the invitation was not entirely altruistic, with the generosity helping to ease pangs of regret for a manager who has exceeded the achievements of any of the players who served under him.

Cooper told me: "We worked our socks off for him and he appreciates that, even all these years later. There were three or four of us that, after playing so many games so young, struggled with injuries that meant we didn't play on for as long as we possibly should have. Myself, Neil Simpson, John Hewitt and Eric Black all had problems to different extents.

"We sacrificed a lot over the years – although we loved every minute at the time, there's no doubt about that. We loved playing for Aberdeen and for the manager, but maybe we were overplayed at times. I think he realises that now, certainly lessons appear to have been learned when you look at the way younger players have been treated at Manchester United – they are very carefully used.

"We had a good career and were desperate to do well for him. I wouldn't swap a minute of my time working under him, I'm sure every other member of that Aberdeen team is exactly the same."

Cooper, now with his 50th birthday looming, admits his body is a wreck. Major operations to help counter knee and foot injuries helped to an extent, but he remains riddled with pain after the exertions of his time at the heart of Fergie's Furies in the 1980s. He was one of the players prepared to run through the proverbial brick wall for the man he describes as the "greatest manager ever" and "best man-manager in the business".

Jock Stein, Bill Shankly, Bob Paisley; according to Cooper, there's only one man who can top the list, not just because of his incredible trophy tally but also because of the ultra-competitive worldwide environment he operates within.

The two had a special bond, perhaps down to Cooper's tender years when he was thrust into the limelight and, more than likely, because of his sheer cheek. With a mean line in Ferguson impersonations, Cooper was one of the few with the nerve to take the rise out of the man with the iron fist. In public Ferguson reacted in typical authoritarian fashion, in private moments he clearly appreciated his young protege's zest for life and fearlessness.

That didn't stop him from ordering the battle-hardened midfielder to sing 'Baa-baa Black Sheep' to the rest of the first team squad as punishment for pushing the boundaries a little too far with his pranks, as Cooper recalls: "He said if I behaved like a child he would treat me like one." You can't say fairer than that, but he added: "I didn't like that but did it anyway because what Fergie said was the law."

Today, the pair can look back and laugh about the good old days together at Pittodrie. Ferguson, ensconced at Old Trafford, and Cooper a fellow manager, albeit down the English grades with Hartlepool, meet from time to time to chew the fat and share a joke.

"He's a good manager, but he's also good company too. I was down at Old Trafford for a couple of games recently, before returning to Hartlepool, and Sir Alex had us back in his room after the game and was on really good form. He knows how to look after people," Cooper said.

The last visit was purely social, but some of the Old Trafford experiences have been therapeutic – none more so than the one which followed his departure from Ross County all those years ago.

Cooper recalls: "He was on the phone straight away, inviting me to come and watch them work for a week or two. I really appreciated it at the time. It was my first job in management and the first time I had left a job, so I took it hard. You come to realise that it's just the nature of football.

"Sometimes when you are out of the game you can count your friends on the fingers of one hand, it's true. It is at times like that you really find out who your friends are and he was certainly there for me, the first to get in touch and offer support. For someone of that stature and profile to take time out and be there for me was really touching.

"To go down and be part of it all for a spell was the perfect tonic. I was able to watch them at work and sit and chat to the man himself, talk things through. It cleared my head and gave me something to focus on. You have to battle through things in this line of work and there's no one better at doing that than Sir Alex Ferguson. He has not always had things his own way, you only have to look back to the first couple of years at Manchester United to see that."

The staying power that Ferguson has demonstrated is an inspiration, with Cooper marvelling at his mentor's stamina.

He said: "I will be lucky if I'm still on the planet at 66, never mind still in football. Fergie will rumble on though. I reckon it's his sheer will to win and the fact football is like a drug to him.

"Fergie would be lost without his day to day involvement in football. As long as he is fit, I can't see him ever wanting to give it up and I'm sure United are in no hurry to see him go.

"Fergie's desire to be the best is also still as strong as it was the very first day I met him when I was a kid. You can see it in his eyes every time he is interviewed on the touchline during United's games."

Cooper still taps into those qualities from time to time, admitting it is a "comfort" to be able to pick up the phone if need be and take advice from the master.

Some of those words of wisdom ensured he did bounce back from his Ross County disappointment, with a little help from a friend, and remains prominent in the game to this day. It is at Hartlepool that he made the greatest impact, on and off the field, with his style embraced by supporters.

It is a style that is unique, with Cooper's happy-go-lucky attitude mixed with a will to win that is such a familiar trait among Ferguson apprentices. He points to his early education at Pittodrie as a key influence in his career to date, not least the way in which he was shown that if you are good enough then you're old enough.

It was in October 1980 that Cooper was told he would be making his Aberdeen debut, with his 17th birthday looming on the horizon.

He explained: "I was cleaning the manager's office as part of my duties around the club as one of the young players when Alex Ferguson came in and told me there was a problem with Alex McLeish and that I had to get myself home and prepare to play the next day. I think a mixture of panic and excitement set in.

"I'm sure my mum thought I was joking when I went home and told her. I was still a young boy – to have gone from growing up in Aberdeen and being a ball boy at Pittodrie to be playing in the first team was special.

"To be asked to step in for a player like Alex McLeish was daunting but once you get out on the pitch all of the nerves disappear. Being surrounded by so many good and experienced players helped and there was no way I wanted to let them down."

He went on to win the Scottish Cup twice, the Premier Division twice, the League Cup, European Cup Winners' Cup and the European Super Cup before his £350,000 switch to Villa.

Cooper added: "I was 16 when I played my first game for Aberdeen, 17 when I scored in the Scottish Cup Final win and 19 when we won in Europe. At the time I took it all in my stride but looking back now I appreciate most players will go through their whole career without those experiences. It meant a lot to me that someone like Alex Ferguson showed faith in me when I was starting out and I'll always be grateful for that. I took it into management with me – I've always believed in giving players a chance at 16 or 17 if they deserve it."

That attitude towards youth is far from the only Ferguson quality that Cooper has attempted to instil in his teams, with the legendary will to win of his former boss another of the traits he himself carried. As Cooper points out, he has "never met another person more determined to win than Fergie" and often had to dodge missiles, including snooker balls and socks, when the post-defeat rage kicked in during Pittodrie games sessions.

He still bears the scars from the flying elbows from training sessions where 'friendly' head-tennis sessions turned ugly, but the warm memories are a great healer.

Cooper added: "A lot of training routines and ideas I use today are the same as ones he introduced to us at Aberdeen. I am sure if you asked Gordon Strachan, Mark McGhee, Eric Black or anyone still involved in coaching they would say exactly the same thing."

And that's the crux of the matter. Like so many touched by their 'friend' Fergie, Cooper was inspired to go on and attempt to recreate, at least in some way, his efforts in the dugout.

Those players Cooper mentions, with the likes of Alex McLeish also in the elite company, were all driven in that direction by their Dons gaffer.

He said: "It is unusual for as many from one team to go into management, but it is no surprise. We were pushed to do our coaching badges while we were young.

"We didn't realise it at the time, but the manager was doing us a huge favour by ensuring we had those qualifications while we were still playing.

"I would far rather have been on a beach in Majorca than slogging it out on the courses over the summer, but I can see the benefit now.

"We weren't forced to do it, but we were encouraged. It benefited us as individuals but it also helped the club – it was like we'd all done a pre-season before we'd even reported back after the summer break, because you're pushed relatively hard while you're working through the badges.

"It wasn't uncommon to look around those sessions and see half a dozen Aberdeen players. We were by far the youngest there, but in later life we would thank him for it."

Many people were influenced by Ferguson during his Aberdeen tenure. Equally, he too had his life shaped by the characters who welcomed him into the close-knit Dons family and played a part in sending him along his chosen path.

One of those key individuals was Teddy Scott. As a player, coach, kit man and supporter he dedicated his life to the Pittodrie club. He worked tirelessly, day and night, for the cause and it was the type of dedication that Ferguson adored.

When Scott, a club legend despite playing just a single competitive match for his beloved team, died in 2012 it was left to his esteemed former boss to lead the tributes as the funeral was held in the Aberdeenshire town of Ellon.

Ferguson said: "Sometimes someone walks into your life and they stay there. You might be a thousand miles away from them but they're always in your thoughts. That's the way I would describe my relationship with Teddy. He was always in my thoughts, even when I left Aberdeen, because when I came here as a young manager he was integral to everything I achieved."

When Scott was awarded a testimonial in 1999, there was only ever going to be one team providing the opposition. So it came to pass that Manchester United, at full strength, travelled north to honour an unsung hero as he marked close to half a century on the staff at Aberdeen.

Speaking at the time of his friend's death, Ferguson noted: "Loyalty should always be recognised and rewarded. All the great heroes that Aberdeen had – the Millers and the McLeishes – they didn't deserve it as much as Teddy did. Because after 49 years you deserve that."

In many ways the two were cut from the same cloth. Both lived and breathed football. Both could be ruthless when need be, but knew when an arm around the shoulder was required. Many of the man-management techniques employed at Old Trafford today can be traced back to the wisdom imparted by the doyen of the Pittodrie boot room.

Ferguson once remarked: "Teddy has been more than just a trainer to Aberdeen. He has been a valued advisor to almost every manager the club had during the first 100 years. I never hesitated approaching Teddy if something cropped up that I felt his wisdom could help sort out. I trust his opinions and a lot of the advice has remained of value throughout my career as a manager.

"His gift is in preparing those young men for life, not just to be footballers. Teddy can be pretty hard on some of the young lads, but he knows what he is doing.

"Being a success as a professional footballer is all about self discipline and a willingness to work hard. Teddy makes sure the young players realise that right from the start, he has been a real father figure to countless Aberdeen players over the years."

He trusted his good friend's judgement on more than just character – he knew the value of his football opinions too. Ferguson said: "If Teddy told me a player was ready to make the step up into the first team I would make it happen.

"There is no one better for picking out when a player is capable of crossing that barrier. That is because Teddy would spend hours helping them iron out weaknesses.

"I recall watching with great admiration as he put a young Alex McLeish through his paces. He had Alex trying to head cross balls away from under the crossbar as he was literally battered into the net by three or four bigger team-mates.

"Poor Alex got a right hammering and must have wondered what it was all about – but Teddy was preparing him perfectly for all the big challenges that lay ahead. Alex became one of the best centre-backs of his generation."

The bond between the two men was strong, but it was not all roses in the garden. Scott was not averse to giving the rising managerial star a piece of his mind.

Ferguson admits: "Teddy was never afraid to do that! He could be particularly scathing if I even treated one of his youngsters too harshly."

The lure of Manchester United's megastars guaranteed a full house at Pittodrie for Scott's testimonial, a rarity in the post-Ferguson era. He returned in 2008 with his team for another testimonial, this time to honour the team that won the European Cup Winners' Cup for him against Real Madrid 25 years earlier.

He has always been willing to offer a helping hand for causes close to his heart in Aberdeen, although surprisingly the flow of loan players between Old Trafford and Pittodrie has not been as steady as you might imagine.

With the exception of Alex Notman, the young midfielder who arrived with great expectation on his shoulder but failed to shine during a temporary posting when he was sent north to try and shore up the Dons in 1999, it hasn't been an avenue that has opened up to Aberdeen.

It doesn't stop current incumbent Craig Brown from trying mind you, with the former Scotland boss admitting at the end of the 2011/12 season that he had been in touch with his club's most eminent former manager with a view to snaring some talent to help push the club back towards the European places. It may just be that having friends in high places may yet pay dividends for the club so close to Sir Alex's heart.

Chapter 15

LONG BEFORE Darren Ferguson was even a twinkle in his father's eye, there was another budding football manager in Clan Ferguson of Govan. Martin Ferguson, brother of Alex and so close they were even born in the same year, has been in the shadow of his illustrious sibling for decades but has had a part to play in his success.

Martin is best known as a key cog in the Old Trafford machine, having served as part of the global scouting network since the 1990s – and presumably having had an input in some shape or form long before then. One of his earliest official recommendations was the signing of Uruguayan star Diego Forlan while the likes of Jaap Stam and Anderson were others from the same scout's notebook. More recently, the pursuit of hot property Eden Hazard, ultimately a race lost to Chelsea, was part of Martin's remit.

Credited with an encyclopedic knowledge of players across the planet, he has been a key ally – even if his role within the hierarchy has drawn accusations of nepotism from small sections of the Manchester United support.

In truth, Martin's background in football is not totally removed from that of his famous brother. He was a time-served welder at the Fairfields' shipyard but also a notable player, winning the Scottish Junior Cup with Kirkintilloch

Rob Roy and going on to play professionally. He was one of the junior game's hottest properties and was watched by the likes of West Ham, Aberdeen, Brighton and Dundee before plumping for an assignment in Glasgow with Partick Thistle.

Spells with Morton, Barnsley and Doncaster followed. It was then that his managerial ambitions rose to the surface, with his appointment as player-boss of Irish side Waterford at the tender age of 25 in 1967. He had just a single season with the club, but is still regarded as a legend to this day.

His one hit wonder comprised winning the championship and reaching the FAI Cup Final by blending local talent with star imports, such as England international John Matthews, before a fall-out with the board saw him return to Scotland and slip back into his role as a player and winding his way back to junior football with East Kilbride.

He was handed a coaching role by Albion Rovers before breaking out on his own again as manager of East Stirlingshire. Remember them? Martin took charge of Shire seven years after his brother had cut his teeth at Firs Park but faced familiar problems, with a threadbare squad and barely enough money to scrape together a starting 11. It was the school of hard knocks, but he attacked it with the familiar family work ethic and would take time out to visit his brother at Aberdeen to take tips from the revolution that was happening at Pittodrie.

Martin, who had also coached with Albion Rovers, was, like Alex had been, part-time with East Stirling. His day job was as a sales rep peddling welding rods – life as a globetrotting employee of one of the world's best known football clubs was not even a distant dream, it was total fantasy. Yet, in time, it became reality.

In those early days with Shire, he extolled the virtues of a shared football philosophy with his brother – who was in the process of building the team that would win silverware in Europe. He said he hated negative football, claiming the only time he sent his East Stirlingshire troops into battle with a defensive battle plan resulted in a 6-0 thumping. He and Alex were two peas from the same pod.

Martin went on to serve as assistant manager to Alex Miller at Morton, St Mirren and then Hibs. Miller would himself become a worldwide scout of some repute for Liverpool, as well as serving as assistant manager with the Reds, as the two followed a similar path.

No stone has been left unturned in the pursuit of talent, with Nemanja Vidic among the finds. But Martin has never been afraid to go back to his roots, with John O'Shea recruited from Ireland thanks to a connection fostered through his Waterford contacts. The old boys network is still going strong and the Ferguson family's links are many and varied. What they all benefit from is a common respect among the football fraternity.

Neil Cooper heads the youth development department at Aberdeen Football Club now. He himself emerged through the system at Pittodrie, before going on to play for the first team – including under Alex Ferguson in the late 1970s and early 1980s. He is also one of the few to have served under Martin Ferguson, later in his playing career.

Cooper told me: "I worked with both of the brothers, with Martin at St Mirren and then Hibs working under Alex Miller. Drew Jarvie was part of Alex's team, so he worked closely with Martin.

"It's impossible to compare the two brothers, primarily because Martin was part-time. He had a good job outside of football. Regardless of that, with Ferguson there is no comparison – particularly when you look at the huge success he had with Aberdeen.

"What I would say is that Martin is a good football man, there's no doubt about that. He knows his way around the game and is a nice guy into the bargain.

"He coached at a decent level in his own right and that doesn't happen if you are not up to the task.

"In his current job with Manchester United there's no hiding place. If you make a bad signing there then the whole world knows about it, so he is clearly doing a good job. There is no way you can last in a job with a club of that scale without success in your role."

Cooper, who had been a prolific goalscorer as a teenager but was switched to defence after joining the Pittodrie staff, made his debut three years before Alex Ferguson checked in at Pittodrie. He played a support role to Willie Miller and Alex McLeish before Ferguson agreed to his departure in 1980, with a move to Barnsley lined up. He returned to Scotland to play for St Mirren, via a stint at Grimsby, and was part of the Buddies' 1987 Scottish Cup-winning side. He moved to Hibs two years later and spent two years in Edinburgh before returning to Pittodrie to play his part in the club's development as a coach at reserve and youth team level.

Far from shying away from the Ferguson legacy, Cooper would love to recreate his former manager's golden touch.

He said: "People say you go back to the Gothenburg team for inspiration and to an extent that is true. What Alex

Ferguson, Archie Knox and Teddy Scott did together was build a team by making the best of the good young players the club was producing at that time. The difference was that if he needed to go out and spend £100,000 on a top level player, he had the option to do that. It simply isn't the case any more.

"What we are trying to do is very similar though. We want to maintain our reputation as a club that is good at bringing young boys through and giving them a chance. We have a good youth policy and are able to attract talented players to be part of that.

"We have seen in recent years quality young players coming through to first team level and hopefully that will continue. You can only do so much for any player – a lot has to come from within – but our job is to make sure they fulfil their potential."

So the mantra lives on. Just as Ferguson paid great attention to rearing the best young talent, so too are the men trusted with attempting to in some way drag the club closer to the high standards set by the main man. Those who were on hand to witness his early days at Pittodrie recall him making the tortuous journey from the east coast to the west of Ayrshire to watch the Aberdeen Secondary School Select play in a Scottish Cup Final. He was fresh in the door and up to his eyes in admin duties, but Ferguson saw it as part of his remit to pile on the miles in his pursuit of the best players, young or old, to help him fulfil his ambitions.

He did, naturally enough, rely on the eyes and ears of others to help him out. In *Managing My Life* Ferguson addressed the qualities of his ideal scout when he said: "Obviously he should be able to judge a player but when the quarry has been identified the scout must ward off the other pursuers, and that calls for resourcefulness, perseverance and often a little low cunning. All of those attributes, and a few more, were conspicuous in Archie 'Baldy' Lindsay, who did wonders for me at St Mirren and was perhaps the most remarkable of the countless scouts I have used during my career in management.

"Baldy was a taxi driver from the Kinning Park district of Glasgow and he had made a name for himself as manager of a well-known juvenile team called Avon Villa. My relationship with him was nothing short of tempestuous, frequently punctuated by the weeks of estrangement which followed one of his storming exits."

But he knew the value of good scouts, and bridges would be mended. He still does appreciate that role – particularly now he has even less time to get out, meaning his brother Martin's part in the structure is more crucial than many might imagine.

Martin, in an interview with *The Scotsman*, said: "Stam would be the first big player signed on my recommendation, although I think Les Kershaw [United's former chief scout and Academy director] saw him play first," he said. "I watched him a lot, because, to be honest, I wasn't sure about him, considering the money they were asking. I told Alex at the time I wouldn't pay the £10m, a lot of money at the time. I said I'm not sure, because when he's playing as a twin centre-half against one striker, he looks uncertain, he doesn't like not marking, not having somebody to target.

"Then, in two games I watched him, he was absolutely brilliant, and one of them was at right-back. It was PSV v

Ajax at the end of the season, a league decider. PSV had to win and Ajax scored very early. The PSV coach waited 20 minutes, then moved one central defender into midfield, left Stam on his own between two full-backs and he was unbelievable.

"Van Nistelrooy was another. At the time, I was watching other players at PSV. I'd seen him play for Heerenveen when he was younger, a day I was looking at a goalkeeper. It was a muddy pitch, like an old-fashioned Scottish Cup tie. I didn't know who van Nistelrooy was, but I liked him. I asked our Dutch contact, 'Who's the number ten?', but he said, 'No, he isn't Man U material.' I said, keep your eye on him anyway and let me know how he develops.

"I was doing the whole of Europe myself at that time and couldn't cover everything. Next thing I know, van Nistelrooy has gone to PSV and I told Alex what had happened with the agent in Holland and how he hadn't done as I'd asked. We could have had Ruud long before we got him. I went back to watch just him one night – by this time we knew they were looking for £17m – and I knew right away he was the one. I phoned Alex right after the game and said you just have to pay the money.

"Anderson? Alex had seen him for just 45 minutes and liked what he saw, so I went to see him when he came back from a bad injury. Porto were playing Boavista in the local derby, a good match to see him in. He came on at half-time and it was enough. I phoned Alex after the game and said 'you'll have to sign this boy'. I said, 'I'll tell you, I think he could be as good as Rooney.'

"You won't be surprised to hear that he replied: 'Are you off your effing head?' But I think he could, in terms of influence, be as good as Rooney. He plays a different position, but that night he just really excited me. He came on and changed the entire pace of the game. You don't often get that from one player and there are times when you should go with your instincts, rather than waiting and making absolutely sure by watching him over a long period.

"When people you've recommended do well, it's a marvellous feeling. So, despite the travel, the lack of sleep and having to put up with my big brother, the job does have its moments."

Those moments, according to Martin, can be terrifying. It is not all business class and VIP lounges for today's global scout.

He said: "When scouts like me go to matches, we're not given VIP treatment, sitting in the directors' box or enjoying corporate hospitality before and after the game. More often than not, we're stuck in a seat beside fans and we can become involved in some of the mayhem.

"I got hit twice with bottles in Milan. I kicked up a fuss and, to their credit, they've made sure things have been better there since. It was a match between Milan and Juventus and I was put in a corner, close to the away fans and right below the home supporters on the upper tier. They were throwing the missiles down on us from above. Italian supporters can be pretty wild at times.

"I had also been hit with bottles in Athens. It was a local derby with Panathinaikos and Olympiacos and bottles, seats, you name it, everything was getting thrown. But the last time I went to a derby game, they had stopped allowing visiting fans in. I don't know if that was a permanent or a temporary arrangement, but it shows how bad it was when they saw the need to ban the away support.

"Another time, I was involved in a riot in Brazil, at the Maracana Stadium in Rio. A guy who works for us in Sao Paulo came to meet me and we went to the game in a taxi. Rio can be a wild place too, and it's recommended that you book the cab through the hotel, who then have a note of the driver's number and they know what action to take if anything untoward happens. You even pay the hotel in advance so you don't get ripped off.

"Well, near the stadium, the traffic, of course, just comes to a halt. So we decided to go the rest of the way on foot. The stadium, being huge, looks close, but, of course, it's further away than it looks. As we're walking towards it, a mob suddenly appears out of a side street. The game was between Flamengo and an Argentine team in the Copa Libertadores.

"There were hundreds in this gang, waving huge banners, shouting and bawling. A bit up the road, another mob comes out of another side street, Flamengo fans. Well, next thing you know, war has broken out. The police arrived, wielding these long, whippy sticks, and if you get in the way of them, you won't half feel it. People were ducking and diving all over the place, including us, running for their lives, while others were carrying on fighting. People don't understand how demanding it can be. People may think my job is something of a jolly, but it can be very demanding."

But then, meeting demands has never been an issue for any branch of the Ferguson family tree. The shipyard heritage has much to be credited for and the younger members of the clan, brought up in privileged position, has inherited the same sense of identity that spurred Alex and Martin to make their way in the world.

Sons Darren and Jason both followed their dad into the game, Jason as an agent and Darren as a player and, in more recent years, manager.

Both have undoubtedly benefited from their father's position in the game to give them a foothold in their respective professions, but both have also suffered as a result.

Jason, notoriously, found himself in the spotlight in the 2004 BBC programme *Fergie and Son*. Designed as an exposé of Jason's dealings with United and United players, the show provoked a furious response from the family – who angrily refuted any suggestion of wrongdoing, leading in turn to Ferguson's rigid boycott of the corporation for more than seven years that followed. He described the BBC as "arrogant beyond belief".

It was a high-profile and impeccably maintained show of solidarity with his boy, as you would expect. But the bond extends far beyond father and son, as Darren explained in an interview with *FourFourTwo* magazine. He said: "He won't mind me saying this – my mother brought us up, he wasn't there a lot because he worked hard.

"I have to say there's no way he would have the success he has without my mother – there is no doubt about that.

"His determination and desire to keep on churning out teams is the thing that's made him different to anyone else. He still gets up early, gets into work early, probably before most people."

Darren's playing career, first with Manchester United under his dad and then with Wolves and Wrexham, led him down the path of continued employment in the game through coaching. A chip off the old block? Certainly his man-management skills are a familiar strong point, but he's adamant he's his own man.

In an interview with the *Guardian*, he said: "Look, I learned lots of things from my dad, there's no doubt about that, and yes, I have been on courses and all the rest of it, but I just think it comes quite naturally to me. I can make decisions and it doesn't bother me if it affects people or upsets them. Don't get me wrong, I've got a human side too: it's never nice upsetting anybody, but I'm not afraid of making decisions."

Darren has had to make big decisions, none more so than turning his back on Peterborough in 2009 – the club he had led to back to back promotions into the Championship, establishing himself as one of the English game's brightest young managerial talents.

It was a move back to the north-west, with Preston North End, that turned his head. The Preston experience was a salutary one and, in 2010, he found himself out of a job and winging his way back to familiar surroundings to take the helm once again at the Posh and steer them back to the second tier after their drop to League 1 in his absence. Incidentally, Sir Alex was not a spectator at the play-off final that clinched that latest promotion – steering clear for superstitious reasons. Quirks aside, he is a useful source of advice for a man still learning the ropes as a boss.

Darren admitted: "I speak to dad a lot about management. I would be stupid not to. I wasn't sure about what he would say about me coming back to Peterborough but he said, 'It will be a good move for you.' He knew that I had enjoyed success here.

"When I went to Preston, it did not feel right – I knew I had made a mistake, even though I took the job.

"I was actually offered the Preston and Sheffield Wednesday jobs on the same day. It was a case of wrong place, wrong time. It is a shame they made the decision for me to leave as we had only lost one game in five. It was one of those things but it was great to get another chance here.

"When I left Peterborough the first time, it was a case of stubbornness between myself and the chairman. We both could have done something about it to stop it but we didn't.

"You gain from experience. If someone puts money into a club you have to respect their opinion. Maybe I should have respected it a bit more than I did last time."

Respect and discipline are qualities that the Ferguson brood were brought up to display, it is part of the genetic make-up.

What Darren also appears to have had instilled in him is the ability to make crucial decisions at crucial times. Preston, he believes, was a blip – but he has shown a determination not to let his heart rule his head in the future.

That includes ruling out the potential for a return to Aberdeen, the city where he grew up as his father helped the team to unparalleled success. And that's the nub of the matter – in typically cool and calculating fashion, the Ferguson nose for an opportunity is quick to sniff out the fact the Dons' best days are behind them.

Darren said: "The thing at Aberdeen is never going to happen again. That's just the way football has gone. The success they had, in Europe as well, is one of those things that may happen once, but very rarely does it happen twice. I don't know if I could ever see myself managing in Scotland."

He describes Aberdeen as a "good city" where he has a lot of friends, having arrived as a five-year-old and departed ten years later as his school years drew to a close. Like Premiership star Shaun Maloney, he's an FP of Cults Academy in the leafy west end suburb of the Granite City.

He went from that relatively comfortable existence to being thrown in at the deep end, moving lock, stock and barrel as a teenager with his family to unfamiliar surroundings in the 1980s. He passed the test and emerged as one of the crop of youngsters to make the breakthrough at Old Trafford in the years that followed, before going out in the big bad world to make a name for himself away from his famous father.

His career in management, he insists, hinges on looking forward – not back to his dad's achievements: "I like to do things my own way and have my own identity. My name is never going to change. I ask my dad for advice when I think it is needed – but I am no different to anyone else."

Chapter 16

SIR ALEX FERGUSON has been raised to god-like status by supporters and, to an extent, the media. He is the man who has pulled off master-strokes – spending wisely and, in comparison to so many, sparingly to blend home-grown stars with quality additions. But it does not always go right. Even the great can get things wrong. Admittedly the good signings have outnumbered the bad by quite some considerable margin, but it would be wrong to consider Ferguson as a flawless genius who cannot be faulted in his transfer dealings.

Where errors in judgement have been made, quite often the root has been at the manager's door. He has been guilty of being overambitious at times, or perhaps overoptimistic. Whether believing he is the man to unlock the potential that others have failed to, or his is the club that can get a previously injury-hit star back playing regularly, he has been guilty of taking risks that have not paid off. What else would you expect of a racehorse owner?

Just as some of the highest profile businessmen in Britain have black marks against their record – even Richard Branson's fledgling empire was on the brink of going to the wall during his early days in commerce – so to does Sir Alex. Football's a game a percentages and he has taken gambles where others would not, a factor that is perhaps as much a part of his success story as any of his many other traits and qualities.

The difference today is that every signing is scrutinised at close quarters. In his early days in Scotland he was able to dabble in the transfer market with less pressure, free of the 24-hour media culture that envelops everything Manchester United today. The stakes, of course, were far smaller as he worked with a comparatively tiny budget – but it is worth recognising that he was afforded funds to break transfer records while at Pittodrie, so he was playing with funds that were significant and especially so for a club with a reputation for being particularly frugal and well run. Squandering cash would have been frowned upon by a wily chairman and his board.

Nowadays it is a global group of power brokers he has to satisfy and justify his spending plans to, but the ethos has apparently changed little over the years. Ferguson is a man willing to spend big when needs must or the target is delectable enough to merit it – but he's as happy searching for bargains, for blind-side signings, as he was in his time as a part-time boss at East Stirling. The thrill of the chase for a £25 a week player was no different to that of a £25m man.

The occasional weakness has been an unwillingness to admit defeat, to cut the losses when a signing has not worked out. That, after all, would mean owning up to a managerial blunder and football's knight is not prone to that. In time he has held his hands up to the occasional, very occasional, clanger. The one that ranks in his own hall of shame as the worst of them all stems back to 1988.

What was it all about, Ralphie? That's the question many Manchester United supporters of a certain vintage have asked. The recruitment of mercurial Scottish talent Ralph Milne in 1988 has been noted as one of the worst ever signings at Old Trafford – including by the manager himself.

Milne in many ways demonstrated Ferguson's incredible confidence in his ability as a man-manager. Milne's talent was not in doubt, at least not to anyone who saw him at the top of his powers for Dundee United in the early 1980s. He had been blooded in the 1979/80 season by Jim McLean, the hardest of taskmasters, and displayed immense pace as well as mesmerising skill and an uncanny ability to score dramatic goals.

He was a vital part of Dundee United's league-winning team in 1983 but he had tested the patience of his disciplinarian manager once too often and was allowed to leave for Charlton in 1987. He struggled in London and was shipped on to Bristol City, seemingly destined for a life of lower league obscurity.

Sir Alex of Old Trafford had different ideas. He thought he could succeed where McLean, recognised as the other great Scottish manager of his generation, could not and tame Milne's wild ways. His £170,000 move in 1988 was an unexpected second chance, one to be embraced – surely.

The catalyst for the move was not Ferguson directly, but more his assistant at the time Archie Knox. It was Knox who had reminded Ferguson of the talent who had undone their Aberdeen team so many times, the one who suggested that he could be the answer to an attacking dilemma they faced in Manchester at the time.

Milne played just a handful of games, not helped by the fact he was deployed more often than not on the left wing rather than his preferred right flank. But more than that, he had failed to respond to the inspiration Ferguson thought he and the surroundings he was working in would provide.

He had joined the club at a time when the drinking culture of the previous regime was still evident, even if the manager was working overtime to stamp it out, and would be the first to admit he was easily tempted by the trappings of playing for one of the biggest clubs in the country. His place in the dressing room was between Norman Whiteside and Paul McGrath – not considered two of the shrinking violets in the squad of that era, and liquid lunches were part and parcel of the trio's routine according to Milne.

He also had baggage to carry as he arrived at Old Trafford, given the apparent resistance to his recruitment even before he had kicked a ball in the red shirt of United. The Scot was, despite the club's lack of success up to that point, considered by many to be a signing well below the level at which the club should be setting its sights. He and his manager thought opinions could be changed, but circumstances would dictate otherwise as the months progressed.

In his autobiography, co-written with author Gary Robertson in 2009, Milne recalls the drive to Old Trafford to finalise the deal: "A million questions raced through my head, but hardly any were answered. One thing I was sure of, however, was that I wouldn't be overwhelmed just because of who they were. I was always confident in my own ability, always. I actually relished the thought of meeting Alex Ferguson and hearing what his plans were and just where I figured in them."

The answer was on the left wing, the opposite flank from Milne's favoured position. But Gordon Strachan was in his pomp and held the right wing berth, so it was left or nothing for the new boy. Still, he was happy enough with the prospect and ready to give it a go.

Milne went on to make his debut against Southampton at Old Trafford, parachuted in from his previous outings in the Third Division to try and impress a packed Theatre of Dreams. By his own admission, the game passed him by, with United scraping a 2-2 draw at the end of an uninspiring display across the board. It was not the dream start Milne had hoped for after a cool response to his arrival.

Recalling his signing, the winger said: "I was taken to their press room which back then wasn't nearly as plush as it is now, but was still damned impressive. About 20 reporters greeted my entrance. I couldn't believe it. Some of the questions I was being asked were just plain daft. They made a big issue of the transfer fee, indicating that it wasn't a huge amount. For a club such as Manchester United it was peanuts really.

"They latched right onto this and were saying things like 'And where had he come from – a Third Division club?' It felt quite belittling, sitting there listening to that. They were putting me down before I'd even kicked a ball."

It scarcely improved for the former Dundee United man throughout his time at Old Trafford. A loan spell at West Ham, under Lou Macari, was blighted by injury and a long period on the sidelines back at Old Trafford followed. From then on in, it was a point of no return.

He explained: "At this point in my life, my enthusiasm for the game of football had drained considerably. I was asking myself questions about my whole attitude and professionalism towards the game and I didn't have any answers. The old hunger, sparkle and desire had long gone, my inspiration had melted away like the snows of spring and the fire in my belly was extinguished.

"It was probably debatable whether I noticed these things happening or whether I even cared. However, I will state quite frankly, I wasn't unhappy and hadn't retreated in on myself. The circumstances were what they were and I just went with the flow.

"I was very surprised, therefore, when Fergie pulled me in and offered me another year's contract. If I'm honest I really did not expect it to be renewed. Perhaps they'd offered it because I'd been injured and missed five months of the season, who knows, but I was definitely happy to stay. I loved life in Manchester."

The 1990/91 season proved to be the last of Milne's unremarkable Manchester United career, as he continued to struggle for form, fitness and motivation. Dumped down to the reserves, along with ostracised goalkeeper Jim Leighton, he struggled to even turn out for the second string. The chance he had been given two years earlier had been blown as he continued to live the party lifestyle. Ferguson and his assistant, Archie Knox, gave up on their wildcard signing, accepting it was a lost cause.

Milne remains defiant, claiming: "When I look back on my time at Manchester United I don't think I did a bad job, when I was playing that is. I was given an opportunity to play for the most famous club in the world, albeit at a time when they were in obvious disarray. Playing left-wing wasn't my favoured position but I would have played anywhere to get a game.

"I came in for some heavy criticism from a section of the support and have been labelled in some quarters as 'one of the worst signings ever for Manchester United'. To those knockers I will say this – my contributions during those games in which I played were no less than those of my fellow team-mates. The simple fact is the team did not function as a unit and did not gel together."

Not surprisingly, he was released. The £170,000 gamble had not paid off and the manager moved on. The player moved on too, first on trial in Turkey and then popping up as a signed player in Hong Kong's domestic league. A brief stint with Derry City followed before the boots were packed away once and for all, the memories of arriving in Manchester for a potentially life-changing moment nothing more than a fading memory.

The fee paid for the mercurial winger was a mere drop in the ocean for a club of United's stature, but that wasn't the key factor. Supporters, the media, the manager – all had expectations of every player who walked through the front door and anyone who failed to live up to those standards could expect little mercy.

That was the case with Milne, and has been the case with a small band of other recruits who have failed to sparkle. And that number really is miniscule, in comparison to the hundreds of players who have passed through Ferguson's teams in his long and distinguished service.

Ask any Aberdeen fan to name a poor Alex Ferguson signing and they will struggle.

The only one that might provoke a pang of regret is Andy Harrow, a name unlikely to be remembered by many. The Fifer cost £65,000 when he was recruited from Luton Town in 1981 and Ferguson was a big admirer of the all-action striker. He had started his career with Raith Rovers and was expected to return to Scotland with a bang, but it turned out to be more of a whimper. He departed for Motherwell early in his second season at Pittodrie, and went on to shine for the Steelmen. Harrow failed to click with the Dons, but Ferguson was always adamant he had the ability to.

At Old Trafford, Milne was one of the first flops to have been recruited – but not the last. In 1995 there was the contribution of William Prunier to the Red Devils' cause. If you don't remember the name, it is probably because he did not hang around long enough to become familiar.

The Frenchman had been part of the same Auxerre youth set-up as a certain Eric Cantona. Unfortunately, there the similarities ended.

Initially he had arrived on trial at Old Trafford with a view to playing some reserve games, but he was thrust into the first team due to injury problems.

The defender made his debut in a 2-1 win against QPR, playing well, but was torn apart in the following match as Spurs won 4-1 at White Hart Lane. Any hopes of a permanent deal were shattered in the course of a torrid 90 minutes, and he was shipped out soon after.

Maybe a trialist shouldn't be considered as a failed signing, but the fact is he got more first team action than many fully signed members of the squad have done. On that basis, he makes it onto the less than illustrious list.

But not every disappointment can solely be laid at the door of football judgement. Character, that quality Ferguson is so renowned for spotting and fostering, has been an occasional weak spot. The arrival of Eric Djemba-Djemba in 2003, the rising star of the Cameroon national team, was a perfect example. Hailed as the perfect replacement for Roy Keane thanks to his all-action style, the African never hit the heights. His manager hinted at off-field problems contributing to his indifferent performances, but never elaborated. In later years, after he had moved on to Aston Villa in 2005 and then Qatar, tales of wild financial excess began to emerge – along with reports of bankruptcy proceedings on the back of that wild abandon.

His agent claims Djemba-Djemba was at one point running a fleet of ten expensive 4x4s and had a web of borrowing that involved juggling cash in 30 different accounts. He had initially arrived in Europe with French club Nantes, where he apparently expressed wonderment about cash coming from walls – the ATM bug had struck as the big wages began to flow in.

Clearly his focus was not all that it should have been, with the hot young prospect making just 39 appearances for United before Ferguson conceded defeat and let him go on his way.

At an average of just over £1m per calamitous first team appearance, Massimo Taibi was another costly error in judgement. The call was possibly clouded by the desperate need to replace Peter Schmeichel, the rock upon which so much of United's success had been built.

Taibi arrived from Venezia in a £4.4m deal in 1999 with hopes high that he would be a key man for years to come. It didn't pan out that way, with alarm bells ringing when he made a costly error on his debut against Liverpool and then conceded five against Chelsea. A horrendous blunder against Southampton, allowing a Matt Le Tissier effort to roll under him, was another blooper in a four-game first team career that was remarkable for all the wrong reasons.

To this day, his eccentric performances maintain his place as something of a YouTube sensation – but in the most negative way. Taibi was sold in 2000 at a considerable loss, with Reggina ending his Old Trafford nightmare when they weighed in with a £2.5m offer for the jittery shot-stopper and drew a veil over what had been a turbulent time for him in the cut and thrust of the English game.

Taibi's experiences in England shaped his outlook on football and life in the years that followed. Speaking in more recent times, the Italian blamed his manager for his struggles in a United shirt. Taibi claimed: "Ferguson didn't believe in me enough and gave me no time to prove my worth. I needed a period of acclimatisation, and instead I was given none.

"I arrived in the August and was immediately picked to play, even though I didn't know the language or my team-mates well. The Premiership is unique, totally different from other European leagues.

"The biggest regret was that I didn't prepare with the rest of the team and I wasn't able to play in the Champions League. Certainly things could have been different."

Taibi's failure could be laid fairly and squarely at his competency in the matches he played, with a question mark hovering over his preparation for those matches in his eyes. Fellow strugglers have toiled more because of mental application than physical calamities.

Passion, determination, commitment. They are three qualities that Sir Alex Ferguson has always admired in a football player and they were three that were sadly lacking when his side scraped a 1-0 win against minnows Crawley Town in the FA Cup in 2011.

Among that number was winger Gabriel Obertan, who had been recruited from Bordeaux in his French homeland for £3m in 2009. When asked what his players had got out of the experience of playing against Crawley, Ferguson snapped: "Me losing my temper." It was an indication of how he had taken the inept performance and from that point on it looked to be the beginning of the end for Obertan and a handful of team-mates from that match.

Ferguson added: "We had some players who maybe don't understand what FA Cup football is like. For them, that is the biggest lesson. There is no doubt a few players did not do themselves justice."

Obertan was eventually sold on to Newcastle, recouping the initial outlay. He had arrived with hopes of becoming another Gallic hero but left quietly, having made little impact after struggling with a series of niggling injuries which held him back.

While Obertan was untested prior to his arrival, it would be fair to assume a World Cup winner would come with certain guarantees, but in the case of Brazil schemer Kleberson that did not prove to be the case. He had been highly praised by his national team coach Luiz Felipe Scolari after starring in the 2002 World Cup triumph and was unveiled at the same time as Cristiano Ronaldo, having signed in a £5m deal from Atletico Paranaense in 2003. Big Phil claimed: "He was always the first name on the team list, ahead of players like Ronaldo. He will have no problems adapting to the Premiership."

Famous last words. Not for the first time, a South American import struggled to adapt to the pace and power of top level football in England and he struggled to impose himself on the Manchester United team or the domestic scene as a whole. Kleberson was sold to Turkish side Besiktas in 2005 after just 20 appearances for the Reds, with the £2.5m fee leaving the club counting the cost of their experiment.

He had the pedigree, clearly had the ability and also had experience at the highest level of all – but Kleberson and Manchester United simply didn't click.

Indeed, South Americans in general have not always proved the shrewdest acquisitions for Sir Alex of Manchester. A succession of irrefutably talented individuals have been lured to the north-west of England in search of riches and silverware, but few have had significant success. Many have cost huge sums, far less have provided a decent return on that investment.

Exhibit A: Juan Sebastian Veron. It cost a whopping £28.1m to recruit the Argentine star from Lazio in 2001. He had been a standout performer in Italy's Serie A, that toughest of football environments. He was an international star with one of the world's great teams. He had physical presence and athleticism, not to mention the other components the modern midfield player requires. He was, in essence, the perfect man to anchor the Manchester United midfield.

Except he wasn't. Veron struggled to impose himself and, despite some displays worthy of a man of his standing in the world game, did not look like a £28m player often enough to retain his place as the lynchpin of the United team – with Paul Scholes and Roy Keane retaining the key role in the side. He was sold to Chelsea for £15m in 2003, but again found the going tough.

Veron had stayed around long enough to win the Premiership title with United in that year, but when the dust settles on the modern era it is fair to say he will not be one of the first names to spring to mind when considering the greats of the glory years.

Diego Forlan is another who found it difficult to hit his stride in a red shirt. The Uruguayan striker showed flashes of the ability that persuaded Ferguson to take a chance on him, paying £7.5m to lure the young hot-shot from Argentine side Independiente in 2002.

Forlan got plenty of opportunities to shine, a measure of his manager's faith in him, but struggled to grab those chances with both hands. It was after his move to Atletico Madrid in 2004 that Forlan blossomed and proved himself as one of Europe's best striking talents – leading to a switch to Inter Milan in 2011 and rumours of interest from Manchester City after that.

While South America has provided, at best, mixed results, the lure of the Asian continent has also proved too strong to resist at times. Whether coloured by the marketing man's dream of cracking that most enthusiastic of markets or not, Ferguson has not been averse to dabbling. Some you win (Park Ji-Sung), some you lose (Dong Fangzhuo).

Fangzhuo joined at the start of 2004 but had his career disrupted by red tape. When he eventually received a work permit, it appeared not worth the wait as he barely featured.

A cameo in a Champions League tie against Roma, a League Cup tie against Coventry City and dalliance with the top flight in a match against Chelsea proved to be the sum total of the import's contribution to the cause. He was sent out on loan to Royal Antwerp during his time in England, before returning to his homeland in an attempt to rebuild his career.

Naturally, for every disappointment there have been ten impeccable choices on Ferguson's transfer record. For every Fangzhuo there's a Roy Keane, for every Veron a Wayne Rooney and for every Obertan a Cristiano Ronaldo. That trio alone demonstrate Ferguson's ability to pick out young players worthy of heavy spending, not scared off by inexperience or a hefty price tag if there is a player he feels he can mould into a world-class performer. Which is exactly what he did with Keane, Rooney, Ronaldo and a string of others over the years.

The problem with signing young players is the unpredictability and inconsistency that goes hand in hand with that, a reason undoubtedly for the failure of some to make the grade. Others, regardless of talent, simply are unable to cope with playing for one of the world's biggest football clubs. And some find it impossible to live up to the standards set by the man at the top – perfection is expected, anything less is not good enough.

Chapter 17

WHEN FABIO CAPELLO turned his back on England in 2012, the clamour to guess who would be his successor began. The attention immediately turned to Harry Redknapp, the popular choice not just because of his cheeky-chappy persona but equally because he was the form manager of the moment. Oh, and he's an Englishman. The FA chose to head in a different direction, with the more pragmatic appointment of Roy Hodgson, the other obvious home-grown option.

When Alex McLeish and then Walter Smith walked away from Scotland in the years prior to the Ukraine and Poland showpiece, the chiefs at Hampden were left with the same proposition as their counterparts at the FA. Where to turn to?

The standout Scottish manager of his generation and, arguably, of all time is Sir Alex of Old Trafford. Did the SFA beat a path to his door? Not a chance. The prospect of Ferguson managing the national side is not an idea even the most ardent member of the Tartan Army would countenance, not even in their wildest, haziest, post-match dreams. He is, quite simply, above the national team job.

It's difficult to imagine any Englishman being in the same category, too big or too successful to be considered for Wembley's main job. But that's the situation north of the border, where the fiercely patriotic Scotsman does not even enter the reckoning when the time comes to find the next leader tasked with inspiring the country's football Bravehearts. Every supporter would love to see the undisputed godfather of coaching in the dugout, gum in hand, on an international evening at Hampden but the success of Manchester United and the relentlessness of his pursuit of glory with his Old Trafford charges has made it a no-go.

The big question is whether he could be tempted in the future, once club commitments had been laid to one side, to have one last hurrah with Scotland. The SFA did try, in 2008 and prior to the appointment of George Burley, to persuade him to combine club and country roles. That notion was quickly dismissed by their target, who was wholehearted in his commitment to his cause with United.

If the prospect of the man from Govan taking the reins of Scotland sounds fanciful to many, the idea he would ever jump sides and lead England is plain ridiculous. In more than 20 years south of Hadrian's Wall he has never lost his sense of national identity...or his accent. Yet England tried, tried and tried again to make him take on the Wembley challenge. Each time it was flatly refused, when the search was underway for replacements for Terry Venables, Glenn Hoddle and Kevin Keegan.

Ferguson, speaking on Canadian television in 2010, admitted: "I was offered the chance to manage the England team on a couple of occasions but, of course, it was just out of the question. It's a poisoned chalice anyway. I think it's a terrible job, plus the fact that I would have had a tremendous handicap being Scottish; no matter which way you look it, that's important."

The Scotland job surely could not be considered a poisoned chalice, since expectations have been suitably lowered over the years. And the Scottishness he reckons would handicap him at Wembley would be far from that if he went back to his roots. But still, it would seem, the answer is no.

In his own words, he assessed the situation with the following observation: "No, I won't return to international management. When I'm finished here I think I deserve a rest."

But there's only so much gardening a man can do, so many golf days or outings to watch your prized racehorses in action. How long before boredom sets in and the temptation to get back on the training field proves too strong to resist?

What makes the Ferguson case different is the fact he has already been there, done that and worn the sombrero. It is easy to think of him simply as Alex Ferguson of Aberdeen and Manchester United, to forget the fact he has done what so few managers of his generation have and taken an international side to the World Cup finals.

Perhaps the passage of time is to blame, maybe it is the unremarkable showing of his Scotland charges in the 1986 showpiece in Mexico that had led to the glossing over of that particular section of his career.

Even as an ambitious young manager, the Scotland job was not one Ferguson had sought out. The death of national team boss Jock Stein, who he had so ably assisted, had led to the invitation he simply could not refuse. He had a duty to take charge as the country mourned one of its football legends, a man who had always been there for his young assistant.

In an interview with the *Herald*, Ferguson said: "When wee Jim McLean gave up the job as Jock's assistant with the national team I was praying the Big Man would phone me. I needed something extra as a manager and there was no-one better qualified than Jock to provide that so when he did ring up I grabbed the chance.

"Jock had a bigger intelligence network – he certainly had far more spies – than the CIA and the KGB put together. He knew everything that was happening before it happened. He used to phone me on a Friday night and casually ask, 'So how are things going up in Aberdeen?' And by his tone of voice it was as though he was saying, 'You might as well tell me because I know anyway.'

"And I'd tell him the lot, I poured it out. 'Well, I've made a bid for Billy Stark at St Mirren because it looks as though wee Strachan will be leaving in the summer.' And Jock would reply, 'Good, good, I was going to advise exactly the same thing...'

"Like all great people, he was blessed with deep humility. I was young and eager to learn, so I'd quiz him about his various tactics in Europe. Jock, who'd out-thought everyone, was totally matter-of-fact. 'Ach,' he'd say, 'wee Jimmy was brilliant that night,' or, 'Murdoch was fabulous', never, ever a word about his own role in making the Lisbon Lions champions of Europe.

"He never took any credit and that was a great example to me. I think I drove him crazy with all my questions but he was incredibly generous with his knowledge. Jock could be serious but he could also be great fun and we'd often sit up until two in the morning in a Scotland team hotel where he'd regale me with one hilarious tale after another – invariably involving wee Jimmy Johnstone."

Looking back, Ferguson believes the appointment as manager for Mexico had a detrimental impact on his club at the time.

He said: "I enjoyed it with Scotland and it was a good experience but it was difficult for me.

"In November we were top of the league and after I had taken the Scotland job we ended up fourth. We won the double but I think we would have won the treble if I hadn't taken the Scotland job.

"The big difference was that the day after internationals I found myself busy on press calls when I should have been training with Aberdeen. I found it a big problem.

"It was a question of either wearing my Aberdeen hat or my Scotland hat and if you are doing the job you have to do it 100%."

That prompted him to urge caution when it was suggested Redknapp could have combined the England job with his duties at Spurs as the 2011/12 season wound down. It was more out of concern for his managerial colleague than a particular wish to help the Auld Enemy – he does, after all, remain fiercely patriotic.

When asked recently why Scotland produced so many top managers, he retorted: "You say this as if it's a country that shouldn't be doing well. You forget we actually created everything in this world. I'll give you a book about it, *How the Scots Invented the Modern World*. It's a fantastic book. You shouldn't be surprised."

If the build-up to Mexico 86 was negative for Aberdeen, from a Manchester United perspective it was overwhelmingly positive.

What very few people knew at the time was that behind the scenes there was far more going on for the Dons and Scotland coach than most could comprehend.

Not only was he juggling national team and club duties, he was also asked to make the biggest decision in his career to that point.

Arsenal, struggling to keep pace with Liverpool and destined for mid-table mediocrity, dismissed Don Howe. They needed fresh blood and new ideas and they saw the young man from senior football's northern outpost as the ideal candidate.

Secret talks took place in an attempt to lure Ferguson to London and he gave it serious consideration in the spring of 1986. He confided in Walter Smith, who assisted him at Scotland level, and sounded the Dundee United man out about joining him at Highbury.

But the Gunners were desperate for a quick answer and Ferguson, his head in a spin due to World Cup preparations, could not commit. He remained with Aberdeen, George Graham was appointed Arsenal boss and Walter Smith joined Graeme Souness at Rangers soon after.

With one decision, the course of history was changed for Arsenal, for Rangers and for Manchester United as the square pegs of Graham, Smith and Ferguson fell into place in what time would show were the right resting places for each of them.

So the focus could return to the job in hand, preparing Scotland for the task awaiting in Mexico.

The squad took care of itself in many ways. Five members were from Ferguson's own club, Aberdeen, to ensure he felt at home. There could be no claims of favouritism however – Jim

Leighton, Willie Miller, Alex McLeish, Gordon Strachan and Jim Bett were there on merit. He had also worked with Steve Archibald, then at Barcelona, at Pittodrie.

What was just as important to Ferguson was assembling a staff capable of sharing the burden. Archie Knox was a given, Walter Smith an obvious choice. Teddy Scott, his trusted ally at Aberdeen, was enlisted as kit man and to offer his valued input.

That left one coaching role to fill, and the man chosen for the berth was Craig Brown. Coach at part-time outfit Clyde, it was a surprise choice – not least for Brown himself.

Now a veteran coach and former Scotland boss himself, Brown was then a rookie. He said: "I will never be able to repay the debt I owe to Alex.

"Managing your country is the pinnacle for anyone with a passion for football. It's the best job you can get and I'm grateful for the part Alex played in helping me reach that level."

The pair had first met when they played together for Scotland's youth team in the 1950s and went on to face each other in the senior game and then as managers at club level. They first worked together in Mexico.

Brown added: "I have a league championship medal from my time playing for Dundee, which I'm very proud of. I also won two lower-league titles as a manager with Clyde and look back on my record as Scotland boss with a sense of achievement. I was also fortunate to be awarded a CBE for my services to football.

"But as far as I'm concerned the biggest honour of my career was the day Alex called me and asked if I wanted to be involved with Scotland. When the best manager in the world rates you highly enough to trust you with a task like that you have to feel honoured.

"Alex had the whole of Scottish football to pick from. I doubt if anyone was that shocked when he asked Archie Knox and Walter Smith to help out. But I was thrilled that Alex also called on my services because it wasn't something a part-time manager of Clyde could have expected. I would accept and it led to my career going off in a totally different direction."

A chance conversation also led to the introduction of another component to the Scotland camp, again with an Aberdeen link.

Brian Hendry, now in charge of the global AVC Media group, was a young man making his way in the audio-visual industry in the 1980s when he offered his services.

Hendry recalled: "I had met him [Ferguson] a couple of times in Aberdeen before reading in 1986 that he planned to take tapes of Scotland's opponents with him to Mexico when he was caretaker boss of the national side for the World Cup finals.

"It was maybe a bit cheeky, but I phoned Fergie to ask if he realised the tapes he would be taking wouldn't work in the equipment in Mexico. Fergie is a very thorough man. He came back to me within 20 minutes and told me to pack a bag, I was going to Mexico and had to make sure I took everything they would need over there with me!

"That led to a long association with the SFA, Uefa and Fifa supplying them with videos and eventually moving into producing videos of things like coaching courses. I was with the SFA and Uefa from 1987 to 1997 and built up good friendships with former Scotland boss Andy Roxburgh and

Gerard Houllier. We even do a lot of work for the English FA now."

Squad picked, coaching staff selected and technology taken care of – it was off to Mexico.

It was Ferguson's first attempt at running a tournament camp. It was also the first time most of the players had fallen under his charge for an extended period of time. There was trepidation among even the most talented individuals as they prepared for life under the Aberdeen boss.

Charlie Nicholas, who went on to star for the Dons himself, told me: "Alex Ferguson is renowned for his fiery temperament and aggressive style of management. I can remember going out to Mexico and being warned by the likes of Willie Miller and Jim Leighton that the last thing you wanted to do was get on the wrong side of Fergie.

"In fact, I didn't think he was that bad. What we have to remember is Fergie comes from the old school of management.

"You find people who played in the 1960s and 1970s, as he did, have grown up with mental and physical bullying in the dressing room and on the training pitch. It still exists – nowadays we call it sports psychology.

"Ferguson has proved himself to be one of the best in the business in the art of getting the best out of his team by commanding the dressing room. The same qualities have been instilled in his sides over the years.

"When I was with Celtic in the early 1980s, Aberdeen would come to Glasgow and bully teams. Players like Willie Miller, Alex McLeish, Neil Simpson, Neale Cooper, Doug Rougvie and Mark McGhee were not short of talent, but they also had the physical edge. It worked.

"They would come down to Parkhead and frustrate you with guys such as Jim Leighton, Miller and McLeish so solid at the back.

"The home fans would start to get on your back, urging you to attack. When you get drawn in to pushing forward, you are vulnerable and Fergie's Aberdeen team would all too often hit you with a match-winning counter-attack late in the game."

The chemistry between Ferguson, Archie Knox, Walter Smith and Craig Brown was excellent, according to Nicholas. He added: "Walter is a gentleman but, if you get on the wrong side of him, he will let you know. I had five weeks with them in Mexico and they were absolutely fantastic characters – but strong and ambitious."

Nicholas enjoyed the experience of playing under Ferguson. There was respect, but not fear. As the team settled into its surroundings in Santa Fe, there was still time for fun.

Craig Brown said: "You wouldn't expect the Manchester United players of today to play any pranks on Alex – but he hasn't always been so fortunate. When we were in Mexico some of the lads – I've always suspected the ringleader was Charlie Nicholas – decided to have a bit of fun at Alex's expense.

"I was in the hotel room next to his and Alex came through complaining he couldn't get the lights to work. He was fuming and called the reception to get someone to fix them.

"While he was waiting in the dark, Alex had to go to the toilet. Without going into too much detail, his tracksuit got soaked. Alex had been unable to see in the dark when someone had put some cling film across the top of the toilet seat.

"He knew something wasn't quite right. And that was confirmed when the hotel electrician arrived and discovered the lights were fine but that someone had loosened all the light bulbs in his room. Alex was fuming."

Nicholas could never be considered a shrinking violet, but he knew when the time was right for work and play. Ferguson brought him back in from the fringes of the international scene, after a difficult start to life at Arsenal, and put his faith in the talented young star – appreciating his character too.

Nicholas added: "I've always had a belief if I don't agree with something I won't sit and be quiet. In saying that, it never happened in the dressing room. If a manager had something to say I would go away and pick over the bones, rather than challenge it then and there. The principle I always had was if he was right I would take it on board, if I didn't agree then I would say so."

He was also another year older and wiser by that point, having sampled life in London with the Gunners. He has always believed that if more of Scotland's home-grown talents, including Ferguson's crop from Aberdeen, had sampled life in another league then the national team would have benefited.

The Sky television analyst said: "Maybe Scotland missed out through that. You learn a lot by going away, growing up, getting some responsibility."

Not that he blames the manager for that – he did his best for his club by keeping his players together in one tight unit.

Having played under Ferguson, Nicholas has been on the other side of the fence as an observer in his role on television. Nothing he has seen in recent years has changed the opinion he formed of the boss when he fell under his charge in the 1980s, admiring the way he has managed to ride out media storms to retain his place as head of the club and go against popular opinion when required and stick to his guns when it comes to hiring and firing.

Nicholas said: "No player is irreplaceable. For example, a lot of people lost sight of that when it came to David Beckham.

"Yes, it would be difficult to find a replacement. It might cost money and take time. But life would go on, Old Trafford would still be standing and Manchester United would still be a force to be reckoned with.

"Alex Ferguson must have bought and sold more players than any other manager in the Premiership and I doubt he's losing any sleep about any of those. That calmness hasn't always rubbed off on the fans or media in England.

"There was always talk about disagreements between Beckham and Ferguson, but I have no doubt the decisions made at that time were based purely on football matters.

"If Manchester United, or any club for that matter, are offered tens of millions for any player they would be mad not to consider it. In the current financial climate, especially with the Bosman rule, that type of money could bring in three or four top-class players."

Back in Mexico, the tournament was mixed, at best. Preparations went well and there was a talented squad in place, but in a group with the highly fancied West Germans as well as the typically efficient Danish side and a dogged Uruguay there were no easy games. The manager's assessment was that victory in at least one of the ties would be vital to qualify from the group, and he was proved correct.

For his first match of the finals there was a predictable look to Ferguson's team. He opted for Jim Leighton in goals, with the bedrock of Willie Miller and Alex McLeish at the heart of his defence. He had Gordon Strachan's creative promptings in midfield. All four had been heroes for him three years earlier in Aberdeen colours and he needed them to dig deep again now that red had been swapped for dark blue.

There were smatterings of players from other teams, including big personalities in the shape of new Rangers manager Graeme Souness and Celtic captain Roy Aitken. There was Arsenal star Charlie Nicholas and New Firm personalities in the shape of Dundee United's Maurice Malpas and Paul Sturrock. Ferguson's line-up for his tournament debut read: Leighton, Gough, Malpas, Souness, McLeish, Miller, Strachan, Aitken, Nicholas, Nicol and Sturrock.

The Danes came through to claim full points with a 1-0 win in a game which saw Roy Aitken have a goal controversially chalked off, meaning a bad start.

A predictable 2-1 defeat against the West Germans in the second game, despite Gordon Strachan's opener, left qualification unlikely.

Changes were made for that second match. Alex McLeish dropped out after falling victim to a stomach bug, with the dependable Dundee United stopper David Narey stepping into the breach.

Charlie Nicholas and Paul Sturrock were also absent from the starting 11, both out injured. Nicholas had been clattered in the first match by Klaus Bergreen and, according to his manager, looked to be out for the remainder of the tournament while Sturrock too had ligament damage. They were three influential players to lose ahead of the most difficult match of the group stage by far.

Eamonn Bannon – who had appeared from the bench in the match against the Danes – joined Steve Archibald in stepping up to the plate to sample the unique atmosphere of the finals.

The reshuffle looked to have worked when Strachan struck, but the German machine proved too powerful in the end.

The Germans would go all the way to the final, defeated 3-2 by Diego Maradona and his Argentina team, and the defeat against them was not an embarrassment. For the Tartan Army who had travelled in decent numbers to support their team, it was an all too familiar feeling of so near yet so far against one of the world's leading lights, packed full of household names.

It was win or bust time against a Uruguay team more at home in the heat of Mexico than their European opponents. Once again, Ferguson shuffled his pack due to a combination of fitness and form concerns.

From the match against the Germans, out went Maurice Malpas. Arthur Albiston stepped in to take his place. There was no Graeme Souness either, meaning a place for Celtic's Paul McStay. The captain's armband passed from Souness to Miller as Ferguson turned to his Aberdeen stalwart for inspiration in his hour and a half of need – but there was no recall for Dons partner McLeish, despite his recovery from illness.

Bannon and Archibald also dropped out of the equation, with Graeme Sharp making his tournament debut and Paul Sturrock brought back in to feature.

With Uruguay proving impossible to break down, Ferguson threw on reinforcements with 20 minutes to go – turning to the recovering Nicholas and, for the first time in Mexico, the wing wizardry of Rangers star Davie Cooper in a bid to find the key to unlock the opposition defence. It was all to no avail – the three-match campaign ended with just a single point in the bag and a solitary goal to show for the efforts of the coaching team and players.

The opposition needed just a draw to progress. They set about getting it in the most rudimentary of fashions, as a brutal encounter unfolded. They packed their defence and succeeded in keeping Scotland at bay, leading to a frustrating 0-0 draw and a return flight.

For McLeish it was a painful tournament in more ways than one. Revealing the issues behind the scenes, McLeish told the *Mirror* in later years: "Looking back on Mexico, we definitely lacked a bit of self-belief. We suffered a big disappointment in 1986 – and it was a double disappointment for me.

"We played really well against Denmark but lost 1-0 when Preben Elkjaer somehow emerged with the ball after a challenge with Willie Miller to score.

"I was really ill before the next game against Germany and came down with stomach cramps and the you-know-whats. I was in bed for 24 hours before the game and Alex Ferguson took me personally for a fitness test. I had told him I'd be okay, but in the sweltering heat I was gasping for breath after a couple of headers.

"I just wasn't ready and ended up watching the game on television as the boys lost 2-1. I fully expected to be back for the Uruguay game, but Fergie decided to stick with Willie and David Narey. I was raging and fell out with the manager.

"When we got back to Aberdeen I told him it would be best if I left the club. He told me my contract was up at the end of the season and after that I could do as I pleased. I had a year to calm down. As it happened, the boss left after three months for Manchester United."

Ferguson has since lamented the fact he was not "stronger" in the face of the Uruguayan tactics, but in truth the damage had been done in the Denmark game.

Even before then, the omens had not been good. Ferguson had his preparations disrupted by heartbreaking news from home, with the death of friend and Aberdeen vice-chairman Chris Anderson.

He said: "I was in Mexico with Scotland preparing for the World Cup when Chris passed away. I will always remember it because my wife phoned me to tell me what had happened. I had only been up to see Chris just before I went to Mexico. We had won the Scottish Cup and I took it up to his house to let him see it."

Anderson and Ferguson had developed a strong relationship in their time together, before illness curtailed the director's involvement day to day. He was seen as a football visionary and backed his similarly forward-thinking manager to the hilt. His passing knocked Ferguson off his stride, but the show had to go on.

Preparations for the finals were good, but there were areas for improvement that were implemented during future campaigns.

Brown explained: "We all learned a lot on that trip. One important lesson was that you needed to have more than the 22 players you were officially allowed to use when you were at a tournament. Alex liked to organise full-size practice games. But if we had anyone carrying an injury it meant myself, Archie Knox or Walter Smith had to make up the numbers, which wasn't ideal.

"When I took Scotland to tournaments in the future we also included half a dozen Under-21 or youth players to avoid that problem. It also gave those lads invaluable experience."

While for Ferguson the Mexican experience was his last involvement in the international game, for Brown it was the start of a long relationship with the Tartan Army.

He went on to manage the Under-21 team and then the full international side after Andy Roxburgh, well and truly bitten by the bug. If he was asked tomorrow, it appears certain Brown would be on the first train back to Glasgow to take charge of the Scotland team once again. For Ferguson, the invitation would surely be met with a "thanks, but no thanks".

Chapter 18

I F IT is not Manchester United, and it is not Scotland, then it is unlikely to be in football. The future of Sir Alex Ferguson beyond his tenure at Manchester United is difficult to visualise, but it is difficult to imagine it will involve a pipe, slippers and quiet life in the country. The man who has outlasted all of his peers and apparently breezed through the incredible stress and strain of life at the very top of one of the toughest professions in sport thrives on competition, the thrill of the chase.

He is adamant, however, that Old Trafford will be his last port of call as a coach. When a colleague of mine dared to suggest Ferguson may have been tempted by the prospect of taking charge at Rangers alongside his old ally Alex McLeish when the going was rough for his former protege, he snapped back: "I'm finishing once I leave Manchester United, as I have said many times before. That will be my last job in football. I don't need to say any more on it – I'm not interested."

So that's that – football will be a closed book. But whether in sport, in some shape or form, or in business, it is certain Sir Alex will continue to make the headlines. While the veteran manager need never work another day, his track record suggests the next venture will be just around the corner. Football management has been his main livelihood for more than three decades, ever since he turned his back on his fledgling business empire to devote himself to the task facing him at Aberdeen in 1978, but that has not prevented him from dipping a toe in other waters.

From the internet revolution to horse racing and many points between, taking risks has come naturally – retirement will not change that mindset.

He will miss life with his Old Trafford 'family' when that day eventually comes. In an interview with the *Herald* he revealed: "Yes, I love each and every new morning. You've got to otherwise you couldn't go on doing it. I've been very fortunate in all the things that have happened to me so coming in here as manager of Manchester United is a real pleasure; it's a great club – that goes without saying – and despite its size, there's still something of a family atmosphere about the place. I've got a lot of good people around me and do you know what, about three-quarters of the staff have been with me over 20 years now."

Leaving that behind will be a wrench, but there will be new challenges ahead. The spirit of enterprise, one which has seen the wily old fox become a dot-com millionaire in recent times, began in humbler surroundings than the slick boardrooms of the city.

Like so many players approaching the twilight of their careers, it was the licensed trade that sucked in the young Ferguson. Like most things in his life, there were no half measures (pardon the pun).

A short apprenticeship learning the ropes in the Matelot, an East Kilbride boozer that still stands today – now known, rather charmingly, as The C'mon Inn. In keeping with its new town setting, the same town where the Ferguson family had chosen to settle, it was a modern and unremarkable establishment.

His next port of call was the polar opposite. He went back to the area he knew best, snapping up a bar in Govan. It was known as Burns Cottage when Ferguson bought it, with the Paisley Toll Road pub previously owned by Edward Brunton – a young Rolls-Royce driving entrepreneur of the time.

Fergie's, on Paisley Road West, not far from Ibrox and the home of Rangers, was the name given to the new acquisition. The downstairs lounge was christened the Elbow Room, paying homage to a key aspect of his style as a centre-forward.

Ferguson, in *Managing My Life*, wrote: "Since it was located at the junction of Govan Road and Paisley Road West and drew much of its clientele from a dockland area, whatever charms it now had were not rustic. It had once been a thriving establishment, with a reputation for launching musicians and entertainers towards success, but by the time it came under my control its biggest celebrities were the members of the darts team.

"As with everything else I turn my hand to, I worked extremely hard to get the business up and running and that meant a lot of late nights and little time at home. I had taken pains to learn the ropes of the licensed trade and I knew it was one in which there is no substitute for putting in the hours and paying attention to detail."

Cribbage nights, darts and dominoes were organised to draw in the punters – but pub life was not without its challenges for the rookie bar boss and his staff. Rough and ready clientele led to some interesting encounters.

Ferguson, picking up the story in his autobiography, explained: "There had been a whisky heist and a cargo valued at about £40,000 had been stolen and then re-stolen from the original thieves. The result was a gang war which involved my pub. One of my regular customers was a massive man with a face that had seen any number of confrontations, both in the boxing ring and in the street. Somehow the grapevine became alive with the word that the big man was involved in the heist and its aftermath."

The result was a showdown with a shotgun, in which Ferguson's trusted bar manager was unwittingly caught up. He was whisked away on witness protection, never to be seen again.

Shaws Bar in Bridgeton, Glasgow, was also part of Ferguson's early empire. As traditional as they come, a bar had stood on the site since 1849 and some of the best known names in the city's licensed trade had seen their name above the door. It took its name from Hugh Shaw, who had taken over as mine host in 1952, and the moniker stuck – as did the Victorian bar and gantry, which was part of the fixtures and fittings until the 1990s. Like so many watering holes, that part of Ferguson's past is now closed and the site empty.

Shaws was in partnership with friend Sam Falconer. It eventually went into liquidation, while Ferguson was in charge at Aberdeen, after running up considerable debts, with Ferguson laying responsibility at the door of Falconer. By that stage, Fergie's had also been consigned to the Glasgow pub scene's history books.

Ferguson said: "In early 1978, I decided that managing St Mirren, being involved in the running of two pubs and attempting to be some sort of reasonable father amounted to an impossible combination of responsibilities.

"Fergie's had to go. The enjoyment I had once derived from it had been replaced by an almost permanent headache. Maintenance problems were never-ending and a prolonged period of bad stock returns severely reduced my profit margin. On top of those worries, I was sick of having to come home at weekends with a cut head or swollen jaw from trying to keep the peace in the pub.

"Mayhem didn't erupt every week but from time to time a fight would break out and my efforts to quell the disturbance would put me in the middle of it. One night, after a skirmish with a bunch of brothers that featured flying glass and left another bad gash on my head, I returned home to tell Cathy, 'That's it. I'm definitely getting out.' She was relieved."

He may have exited the industry relatively swiftly, but he remains in touch with some of the customers who frequented his first businesses. Indeed, some have become minor celebrities thanks to their Ferguson connection and anecdotes.

Locksmith Alexander Minty – an occasional visitor to his old friend in Manchester, bearing gifts including potato scones and Scottish newspapers – found himself in the media spotlight when the *Guardian* came calling in 2003. Minty, still a regular at the pub, now known as the Angel bar, has nothing but praise for its illustrious former landlord.

He told the paper: "If I owned a pub I would have Fergie behind the bar. He got on great with everyone. He could speak to people and he did everything himself. If anyone missed their bus or had too much to drink he would give them a lift home."

George Edmund chipped in: "It used to be queued out the door, it was one of the best pubs round about. Alex was a good laugh. He used to have fun with the customers."

Minty, once a promising player who had a connection to Ferguson through St Mirren, added: "I call him the guv'nor. He's the greatest thing since sliced bread. I'm a Rangers man through and through but I like Manchester United and all."

The pub itch, however, has been scratched. Sir Alex won't be returning to life as the host. Instead it's the more civilised surroundings of Britain's racecourses that have become a second place of work for Ferguson, with life as a racehorse owner serving as a release from everyday life in football.

As he did in the drinks trade, he has managed to win friends and influence people since first getting involved in the late 1990s. Once time is called on football, it appears certain the adrenalin rush usually experienced on a Saturday afternoon will be recreated by the sport of kings.

It was in April 1998 that Queensland Star, his first horse, made its debut. Newmarket was the venue and the Ferguson colours were pinned to a mount that wore the name of one of the ships its owner's father had made in the shipyards of Glasgow.

Since then the bug has bitten, with Ferguson represented at meetings the length and breadth of the country – including the Grand National.

Leading trainer Paul Nicholls, the man chosen to take the rising racing star What A Friend under his wing on behalf of Ferguson and co-owner Ged Mason, believes racing offers the perfect avenue for his employer.

CHAPTER 18

Nicholls said: "He's just a great enthusiast, he loves it. There's a lot of similarities between racing and football. I've got a squad of players in effect, and so has he. You've always got injury problems and one thing or another. He always says to me that the only difference is that with football players you can talk to them, whereas the horses can't talk to me and tell me what's wrong.

"He totally lets me get on with it. I'll always be ringing him up to keep him up with things, like I would with any of my owners, and he's always phoning me, but at the end of the day, he'd always leave the final decision to me.

"I know what pressure I'm under and it's the same for him. It's a pressure job when you're at the top of your game, but he thrives on it, and so do I."

Ferguson is far from alone as a football man involved in the world of racing, with Wayne Rooney among the celebrity set who have embraced ownership. It is far from simply an expensive hobby – this is big business, with millions of pounds on the line.

That was best demonstrated in 2003 when Ferguson and John Magnier, then Manchester United's biggest shareholder, became embroiled in court action over stud fees earned by Rock of Gibraltar, the legendary horse the pair co-owned.

The friction stemmed from the half share the manager had been gifted, and his subsequent claim for the same percentage of the revenue – with the claim estimated to run into tens of millions. Ferguson later dropped the action, with the parties reaching an amicable settlement over the issue.

With a personal fortune running into tens of millions of pounds, after years at the top in football and shrewd deals

253

in other spheres, Ferguson has a reputation for a ruthless approach to finance. Early in his career he demonstrated his intention to fight his corner, and that trait has remained even as the big money has rolled in.

Property investments are part of his strategy, including backing office developments and ploughing cash into huge asset funds tied up in the sector.

In 2003 he put money into Active Asset Investment Management, a start-up firm designed to take the millions of the rich and famous and invest and manage property portfolios on their behalf. Profits would then be shared among the investors. Those included Gareth Barry and Alan Smith, then of Leeds United. Sir Alex said at the time: "I like to get involved with people who are bright and fresh and hungry with good ideas. You need to have a good touch and the people at AAIM have that."

His interests are wide and varied, far from restricted to 'safe' and traditional areas.

For instance, how many are familiar with his role in the ice tea industry? Few, is the answer – not least since his interest in the niche market is confined to South Africa. When new brand BOS was seeking investment following its launch in 2010, Sir Alex was convinced to take a 10% share in the fledgling firm at the same time as international venture capitalists Invenfin took a 20% bite.

The company crowed about its big signing, with Ferguson himself quoted as saying: "I was struck by the passion of the BOS team, and by the great story underpinning the brand. I believe BOS has amazing potential to become a premier player in both local and international markets."

Reading between the lines, he had also been struck by the money-making potential as he looked for avenues to put his hard-earned fortune to good, and profitable, use.

The man who cut his commercial teeth in the industrial environs of Govan's pubs has not shied away from modern business. When approached to invest in online venture Toptable, the brainchild of Scottish digital entrepreneur Karen Hanton, he took the plunge. Fergie became a business angel, along with other backers including celebrity chef Gary Rhodes.

When the business was sold in 2010 it netted Ferguson £4m for his 11% stake in a company that hadn't turned a profit for the first five years of its existence. Eventually perseverance paid off and the profits mounted, with the concept of electronic restaurant bookings catching on to the extent it was seating more than three million diners across 14 different countries each year by the time it was taken over by US group OpenTable for £35m.

Hanton had, apparently, benefited from tips from a managerial master along the way. Ferguson had told her to look at key positions – the spine of her team, to use football parlance – and strive for excellence in each of them. That included the chiefs in IT and marketing, the equivalent of the centre-half and centre-forward for a dot-com business.

While the Toptable investment paid off in grand style, the internet is not a passion in the way horse racing has become. It was simply an opportunity that had presented itself and was grasped with typical enthusiasm.

Like fine wines, another of Ferguson's great passions in life, football managers get better with age. He has proved that better than anyone. Behind him is his wife Cathy, supporting him through thick and thin throughout his long and varied career in football. Not that she's fanatical about the game that has become central to her entire family's life. Quite the contrary.

Ferguson revealed in an interview with the *Mirror*: "You'll not find a thing about my career in the house. My wife Cathy is fed up with the whole thing. She's unbelievable. I can't even take a football book home. If I bring one in she will say, 'What are you doing with that?'"

The call to inform the Fergusons that they were about to have their first knight in their realm was greeted with a simple response of: "Do you not think he's had enough rewards?"

Mind you, they were old hands at Buckingham Palace honours protocol by that point. He received an OBE after Aberdeen's success in Europe in 1983, then a CBE in 1995 as domestic honours flowed thick and fast at Old Trafford. In 1999 the set was completed with a knighthood.

Ferguson may be a global icon in football terms, but to his wife he remains the same man she was first drawn to when she watched him address union members in his role as a shop steward in the shipyards.

He's quite comfortable with that, and the lack of trinkets at home. He said: "I prefer to think about what's ahead and what next I can achieve. I think that has kept my feet on the ground. I've never got carried away with it."